THE SANTA FE TRAIL
IN MISSOURI

PROJECT SPONSORS

Western Historical Manuscript Collection,
University of Missouri in Columbia

Missouri Folklore Society

Missouri Heritage Readers

General Editor, Rebecca B. Schroeder

Each Missouri Heritage Reader explores a particular aspect of the state's rich cultural heritage. Focusing on people, places, historical events, and the details of daily life, these books illustrate the ways in which people from all parts of the world contributed to the development of the state and the region. The books incorporate documentary and oral history, folklore, and informal literature in a way that makes these resources accessible to all Missourians.

Intended primarily for adult new readers, these books will also be invaluable to readers of all ages interested in the cultural and social history of Missouri.

Other Books in the Series

Arrow Rock: The Story of a Missouri Village, by Authorene Wilson Phillips

Blind Boone: Missouri's Ragtime Pioneer, by Jack A. Batterson

Called to Courage: Four Women in Missouri History, by Margot Ford McMillen and Heather Roberson

Catfish, Fiddles, Mules, and More: Missouri's State Symbols, by John C. Fisher

Five Stars: Missouri's Most Famous Generals, by James F. Muench

Food in Missouri: A Cultural Stew, by Madeline Matson

George Caleb Bingham: Missouri's Famed Painter and Forgotten Politician, by Paul C. Nagel

German Settlement in Missouri: New Land, Old Ways, by Robyn Burnett and Ken Luebbering

Hoecakes, Hambone, and All That Jazz: African American Traditions in Missouri, by Rose M. Nolen

Immigrant Women in the Settlement of Missouri, by Robyn Burnett and Ken Luebbering

The Indomitable Mary Easton Sibley: Pioneer of Women's Education in Missouri, by Kristie C. Wolferman

Into the Spotlight: Four Missouri Women, by Margot Ford McMillen and Heather Roberson

The Ioway in Missouri, by Greg Olson

Jane Froman: Missouri's First Lady of Song, by Ilene Stone

Jesse James and the Civil War in Missouri, by Robert L. Dyer

Jessie Benton Frémont: Missouri's Trailblazer, by Ilene Stone and Suzanna M. Grenz

M. Jeff Thompson: Missouri's Swamp Fox of the Confederacy, by Doris Land Mueller

Missouri at Sea: Warships with Show-Me State Names, by Richard E. Schroeder

Missouri Caves in History and Legend, by H. Dwight Weaver

On Shaky Ground: The New Madrid Earthquakes of 1811–1812, by Norma Hayes Bagnall

Orphan Trains to Missouri, by Michael D. Patrick and Evelyn Goodrich Trickel

The Osage in Missouri, by Kristie C. Wolferman

Paris, Tightwad, and Peculiar: Missouri Place Names, by Margot Ford McMillen

Quinine and Quarantine: Missouri Medicine through the Years, by Loren Humphrey

A Second Home: Missouri's Early Schools, by Sue Thomas

Stories from the Heart: Missouri's African American Heritage, compiled by Gladys Caines Coggswell

The Trail of Tears across Missouri, by Joan Gilbert

THE SANTA FE TRAIL IN MISSOURI

Mary Collins Barile

University of Missouri Press
Columbia and London

Copyright © 2010 by
The Curators of the University of Missouri
University of Missouri Press, Columbia, Missouri 65201
Printed and bound in the United States of America
All rights reserved
5 4 3 2 1   14 13 12 11 10

Cataloging-in-Publication date available from the Library of Congress
ISBN 978-0-8262-1880-3

♾™ This paper meets the requirements of the
American National Standard for Permanence of Paper
for Printed Library Materials, Z39.48, 1984.

Design and composition: FoleyDesign
Printing and binding: Thomson-Shore, Inc.
Typefaces: Minion and Old Claude

CONTENTS

—⟨⟨⟨⟨⟩⟩⟩⟩—

ACKNOWLEDGMENTS
ix

INTRODUCTION
From Civilization to Sundown
The Santa Fe Trail Begins
1

CHAPTER 1
The Missouri Frontier
"To the Boonslick, to be sure!"
7

CHAPTER 2
"As far as we wish to go"
William Becknell Leads the Way
30

CHAPTER 3
Life on the Trail
57

CHAPTER 4
Wagons and Merchandise
on the Missouri Trail
83

CHAPTER 5
The F-A-R W-E-S-T
Missouri Trail Towns
104

CONCLUSION

The End of the Trail

122

APPENDIX

The Language of the Missouri Trail

A Glossary

127

FOR MORE READING

139

INDEX

141

ACKNOWLEDGMENTS

J OURNEYS AND BOOKS are never completed alone. I have been fortunate in my friends and family for their support, faith, interest, and good humor, as well as in the writers, such as Nathaniel Patten and Alphonso Wetmore, who were among the first to embrace the frontier with humor and gusto. The following folks are in many ways, the coauthors of this book: Steve and Kelly Archer, Sara Arrandale, Elinor Barrett, Margaret and Bob Baum, Cheryl Black, cfrancis blackchild, Heather Carver, Larry Clark, James Cogswell, Edith Colman, Linda Cooperstock, Juanamaria Cordones-Cook, Ann Dong, Karen Enyard, Rebecca Graves, Susan Hazelwood, Deb Heairlston, Linda Hein, Brett David Johnson, Angela Kileo, Molly Kodner, Gary Kremer, Penny and Lou Kujawinski, Mary Licklider, Elaine Lawless, Susan Meadows, Christine Montgomery, Connie Pilkington, Shirley Pratt, Cathy Ricciotti, Becky and Dolf Schroeder, Gena Scott, Prisca Shija, Deborah Thompson, Ann Woodhouse, and the staffs of Ellis Library, State Historical Society of Missouri and the Western Historical Manuscripts Collection-Columbia, the Nebraska State Historical Society, the Fort Atkinson State Historic Site (NE), Boone County Historical Society, the Missouri Historical Society, the cast and crew of *The Pedlar,* the Columbia Shape Note Singers, and the Friends of Historic Boonville. Marc Simmons has long inspired those who love the Santa Fe Trail. The folks at the Arabia Steamboat Museum remind us all that history is so much more than dates—it is rubber shoes and buttons as well. Bob Dyer loved the Boonslick and its people—he is sorely missed. Susan Flader prodded, challenged, and inspired me to find the heart in history. Phoebe Nichols supported my book addiction. Arlene Hoose has shared many trails, whether they led to cellar holes, caves, or giant tree sloths. Finally, this book is for Mary Lamb Collins and Margaret Collins Barile, who taught me to laugh.

THE SANTA FE TRAIL
IN MISSOURI

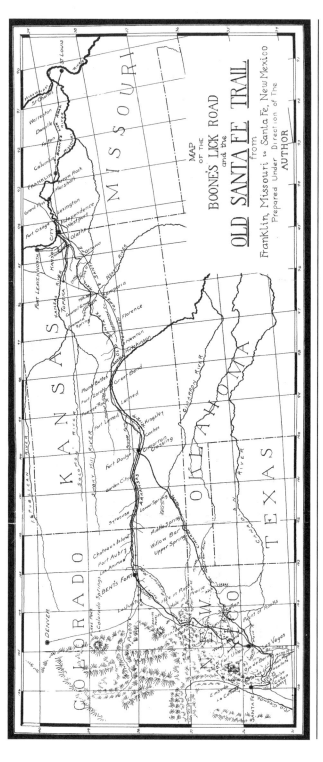

Although the Missouri portion of the Santa Fe Trail had many meanders, cutoffs, and side trails, it generally followed paths formed by Native Americans, early explorers, and trappers. (Map by Waldo C. Twitchell, from *The Leading Facts of New Mexico History*, by Ralph Emerson Twitchell; State Historical Society of Missouri, Columbia)

From Civilization to Sundown

The Santa Fe Trail Begins

⸺⸺⸺⸺⸺◁◦▷⸺⸺⸺⸺⸺

IT SHOULD BE EASY to describe the Santa Fe Trail: it was a nineteenth-century commercial road stretching from Missouri to New Mexico and beyond. Depending on the route taken, the trail was hundreds of miles of rolling, flat, dusty, wet, hot, dry, green, or sandy track crossing Missouri, Kansas, Colorado, Oklahoma, New Mexico. It was home to Indian tribes including Osage, Kaw, Comanche, Navajo, Arikara, Pawnee, Ioway, Missouria, Otoes, Sac, and Fox. But nothing else about the trail is simple to define. It was wagon tracks, narrow in some places, a quarter-mile wide or more in others. Those who "went down the trail" were authors, illiterates, military officers, ne'er-do-wells, adventurers, debtors, and businessmen. The weeks spent crossing the trail alternated between exhausting work, uneasy encounters with Indians, brutal weather, night skies frosted with stars, and a landscape filled with the whispering and rolling of prairie seas.

The Santa Fe Trail experience was nearly impossible to describe, and as difficult and unpredictable as a buffalo ready to charge. For one thing, nearly a half-dozen Missouri towns claimed the trail as their own. First came Franklin, in 1817 the biggest small town west of St. Louis. From here in the cornfields, the first caravans set out for Santa Fe, but as new towns developed, the trailhead moved west, north, and west again. Then in 1825, when Congress authorized a survey of the Santa Fe Trail, mile marker 0 was set at Fort Osage more than 200 miles west of St. Louis. By the twentieth century, historians suggested that the site of the old town of Franklin be recognized as the start of the trail.

But Missouri's Santa Fe Trail stretched east and west far beyond Franklin; in fact, the trail stretched nearly 250 miles across the state from St. Louis on the Mississippi River to Westport on the Missouri. This section, "The Missouri Trail," had a distinct and lively existence of its own. Any Easterner who wanted to reach Santa Fe had to travel the width of Missouri. Some visitors and trail merchants thought Missouri a place of backwoods fools; others saw great beauty in the land and humor in its people. You could dislike Missouri, but you could not ignore it. The Missouri Trail was stitched together from Indian paths, trappers' traces, and wagon roads. It brought explorers and emigrants to the heart of the Missouri territory and then sent them on across the river to the plains. It was the Missouri Trail and then the Santa Fe Trail that offered Americans their first sense of the West with all the adventure, heartbreak, and shame to come. And it was Missourians who first walked the trail and told its story.

The United States had more than doubled its land area with the 1803 Louisiana Purchase, a region once claimed and traded back and forth by France and Spain. While impulsively made (many Americans questioned the right of President Thomas Jefferson to acquire the land), the Louisiana Purchase could not have been better timed. By the end of the eighteenth century, the new nation was already experiencing growing pains. It was clear to some Americans that without land for expansion, the country's growth would be limited. British, French, and Spanish regions surrounded the newly formed United States of America and threatened to stunt the new country economically and politically before it was even out of its infancy. The Louisiana Purchase solved the problem of expansion overnight.

President Jefferson, eager to know more about this new world west of the Mississippi River, sent the Meriwether Lewis and William Clark expedition to travel to the Pacific Ocean and report on the lands and people along the major rivers. Lewis and Clark returned with maps, journals, and stories of encounters with many Indian tribes, who followed a great annual cycle of hunting and camping across the plains, using the rivers for transportation and food. But despite the information that the "new lands" were new only to white settlers, most people in the United States believed it was theirs to claim. Many people—Europeans and Americans alike—took it for granted that since Indians were not Christians or U.S. citizens, they were not entitled to the same rights. Settlers looking for the best lands often pushed into Indian territory to build cabins and start farms before the U.S. government managed to end, or "extinguish," Indian claims to land. U.S. officials attempted to gain title to Indian lands and the goodwill of tribes by negotiating treaties, offering lands farther west or south in exchange, promising to provide trading posts (known as "factories"), providing services of blacksmiths and other skilled artisans, or protecting tribes from their rivals. Many tribes agreed to these "transfers" of land, believing that the U.S. would keep its promises.

The Spanish had explored the upper Louisiana territory as early as the sixteenth century. They established settlements throughout Mexico and traveled east in search of the mythic cities of gold. In 1541, Coronado and his troops marched from the southeast to a region they named *Quivira,* which we now call Kansas. The French claimed the Mississippi Valley in 1682, but by 1762, the Spanish government had received the territory west of the Mississippi from France and wanted settlers to help develop the land. Few Americans had chosen to settle in French or Spanish territories. Not only were there differences in language but, as important, Americans of British origins were often Protestants while the Spanish and the French were Roman Catholics. But Spain had a plan to overcome Americans' distrust of foreign governments. Spanish lieutenant governor Zenon Trudeau invited Daniel Boone and his family to settle near St. Louis.

Boone was the most celebrated frontiersman in America at the beginning of the nineteenth century. But despite a lifetime of trapping, exploring, and settling western lands, despite fame and respect, Boone was nearly destitute by the 1790s. He had neglected to file the proper legal papers for ownership of the Kentucky lands he settled, and the Kentucky legislature refused to recognize his claims. The Spanish granted Boone land and a judgeship to settle in Upper Louisiana and encourage others to follow him, and by 1799 Daniel, his wife Rebecca, several of their children, other relatives, and friends had moved to the Femme Osage Valley near present-day Marthasville. The Spanish guessed rightly that Boone's reputation as an honest man and great explorer would encourage other Americans to follow. By the Louisiana Purchase in 1803, Americans were already settling within the future state of Missouri.

Before the Boones, the earliest white travelers to cross present-day Missouri were French trappers and explorers. These men followed land trails used by Indians, and the even smaller paths, or traces, trampled by animals as they migrated or searched for food. Few maps existed, and those were beyond the reach of the newcomers. But pioneers knew how to mark their traces through the forests. Daniel Boone claimed he had never been lost in the wilderness, only bewildered for a day or two. Paths were indicated by "blazing" a tree, or chopping it with an axe to mark the wood. Stones were piled into guideposts. Groves of trees were used as directional indicators. An unusual trail-marking method left behind a permanent "signpost." Indians and emigrants bent saplings parallel to the ground and tied them in place with leather ties or thongs. This forced the "thong tree" to grow at this odd angle, marking a trail. Some of these trees still exist, pointing the way west two centuries later.

Improvements to the Missouri Trail were not made until well after settlement, when stumps were pulled, brush cleared, and gravel spread on the mud, or wooden planking set down to form a "plank road." If rounded logs were used instead of planks, the road was a "corduroy road," bumpy and noisy for wagons. The logs rotted quickly, so wagons had more to contend with than just mud.

Missouri trails meandered and backtracked on themselves, changed with the weather and with the traveler, but they began to do what they were created to do: bring settlers into the region. In 1804, Daniel Boone's son, Nathan, and a companion were returning from a hunting trip and came across a salt spring 150 miles upriver from St. Louis, opposite present day Arrow Rock. Salt was important to settlers, providing flavor to bland diets and serving as a preservative in a time when ice was available only in winter. The elder Boone encouraged his sons Nathan and Daniel Morgan to start a salt boiling business, and the spring, or lick—so called because animals were attracted to the salt—became known as the Boones' Lick or Boonslick.

The Boonslick settlements were threatened during the War of 1812, but by 1814 the region was the most famous destination west of the Mississippi. The Reverend Timothy Flint, a missionary from Connecticut who lived in Missouri, wrote of the area in 1824:

> From some cause, it happens that in the western and southern states, a tract of country gets a name, as being more desirable than any other . . . the hills of the land of promise were not more fertile in milk and honey than are the fashionable points of immigration. . . . Boon's Lick was the common centre of hopes, and the common point of union for the people . . . ask one of them whither he was moving . . . "To Boon's Lick, to be sure."

BOONES LICK SPRING. SONS OF DANIEL BOONE MAKING SALT.
1807

Discovered by Nathan Boone in the winter of 1804, the natural salt springs that gave the region its name were located near modern Boonsborough. Salt boiling was hot, difficult, and dangerous work—the men were often harassed by Indians, and at least one worker was scalded to death. This mural by Victor Higgins in the Missouri state capitol shows one of the salt kettles—which still may be seen at the Boone's Lick State Historic Site. (State Historical Society of Missouri, Columbia)

Encouraged by reports of fine land and opportunity, and despite the hardships of settlement, the area thrived. Farms sprouted on the fertile Boonslick river lands. Settlers founded Boonville and Franklin more than 150 miles upriver from St. Louis. The towns faced one another across the Missouri River, with Boonville on the southern bluffs and Franklin on the northern prairie. By 1819, soldiers from forts along the upper Missouri stopped at the settlements on their journeys up- and downriver. A newspaper with the grand name of the *Missouri Intelligencer and Boonslick Advertiser* was established by Massachusetts native Nathaniel Patten in 1819. It reported stories of happenings along the river and from back East and as far afield as Europe. Families built cabins and claimed the lands. The first steamboats chugged their way under the river bluffs: one, the *Western Engineer,* had been designed to resemble a sea serpent, with steam billowing from the creature's mouth. Although the ship was meant to frighten Indians, both settlers and Indians gathered along the river to watch the commotion. Mills, taverns, hotels, and shops provided goods, including plenty of whiskey and rum. The Boonslick bustled.

From Virginia, Tennessee, and Kentucky, men like Thomas Hart Benton, a future Missouri senator, the Binghams, Becknells, and Hardemans came to Missouri. From Vermont, Massachusetts, Connecticut, and New York came scholars, preachers, and businessmen. The region had become the Territory of Missouri in 1812, with a delegate in Congress. Only attaining statehood remained, and petitions for statehood began in 1817. It was not until August 10, 1821, however, after a long series of negotiations and compromises, including the compromise allowing Missouri to remain a slave state, that statehood finally arrived.

But despite its successes, Missouri had financial problems. A national panic in 1819 had caused many banks to shut down or default, leaving customers without funds. Banks were not regulated by the government, nor did they offer customers insurance for their deposits. In addition to hard money—coins in gold and silver—the United States had many different types of currency. States issued their own coins. There were dimes, dollars, half dimes, half pennies, all raising questions of value for the merchant and buyer: did the coin actually contain five dollars' worth of silver? Had it been "trimmed"? To prevent trimming, coins were "milled," leaving tiny ridges at the edge. A trimmed coin lost its edges, a clear sign that metal had been shaved off and the coin contained less silver or gold. Was the coin "cased"? This was when a counterfeiter dipped a copper coin in silver and passed it off as solid precious metal. Uncertainty spread, and in a short time, Missouri's two banks failed, and people lost their savings and business capital. Senator Thomas Hart Benton suggested the state base its economy on the value of the silver and gold, and not on the face value of paper currency. His push for this earned him the nickname "Old Bullion," a word for metal money.

In Franklin, the bank failures meant businessmen faced heavy debt. Most of the shops had purchased goods from back East on credit, paying interest on the loan until the merchandise sold. Merchants could not afford to have a farmer barter tobacco or hemp for a barrel of flour; everyone needed hard cash to pay debts. The financial crisis trickled down from banks, to wholesalers, to merchants, to farmers. Among the early settlers who faced financial ruin from the economic problems was a Southerner named William Becknell, who was to become the "Father of the Santa Fe Trail."

CHAPTER 1

The Missouri Frontier

"To the Boonslick, to be sure!"

⟡

FRONTIER LIFE WAS NEVER SIMPLE, comfortable, or secure, and it took skill, strength, and imagination to survive. The men and women who settled along the Missouri Trail had very different stories: some were "dirt poor," arriving in the Boonslick with only a wagon, an axe, and some hope. Others were from modest origins back East or down South and brought with them some "housen" goods, furniture, and livestock. A few, like the Sappingtons and Hardemans, who settled in Missouri before it became a state, were wealthy Southern landowners who built new plantations and ran them with slave labor. Whatever their beginnings, as the emigrants began to shape the frontier landscape, it was just as certain that the frontier changed them. The Missouri Trail was not just travel: it was homes, families, and towns. A look at the Boonslick in the early years of the Missouri Trail reveals much about why the Santa Fe trade succeeded.

Stephen Long was headed upstream to the Yellowstone River in 1819, part of a government scientific expedition charged with exploring the upper Missouri. When Long arrived in Franklin he noted that there were approximately 120 cabins in the town and that they were located in the flood plains of the Boonslick. He was unimpressed with the town's setting and not much more impressed with the town. Long did not offer details about the cabins at Franklin, but fortunately, one traveler that year did. Reverend John Peck was a Methodist minister from New York who traveled through early Illinois and Missouri settlements. He met Daniel

Boone and left vivid descriptions of life in Missouri. Here is what he thought of one cabin only a few miles above Boonville and Franklin:

> Seeing smoke at a little distance from the trail we were pursuing, we found a cabin, about twelve feet square, made of such rough black jackpoles . . . with a sort of wooden and dirt chimney. Very little "chinking and daubing" interfered with the passage of the wintry winds between the logs. . . . The floor was earth, and filthy in the extreme; and the lodging-places of the inmates were . . . scaffolds around the walls, and elevated on forks.

The "black jackpoles" were logs from the blackjack oak, a fairly small, straight tree that thrived in the Missouri clay and sandy soils. A single man could build a cabin if he had enough timber and an axe—a cabin's height was limited only by the strength of the builder. It was difficult for a man to raise a cabin by himself much beyond six feet high. It was also dangerous, since the logs could roll back and crush him. If a settler had neighbors to help, then a cabin could be built in a day during a cabin raising, or "bee," as work parties were known.

At least one Missouri settler, William Brown, had made his life on the frontier easier: he put his homesite at the base of a bluff. Then he chopped down trees and rolled them downhill. This also made getting firewood much easier. Later, when the firewood above his cabin ran out, it was easier for him to build a new cabin than haul firewood to the old one!

To begin a cabin, the builder cleared away brush and chopped down and rolled four large trees into place for the foundation. If there was time before winter set in, the next step was to build corner foundations of flat stones that raised the logs off the ground. This offered some ventilation to keep the logs from rotting. It also provided a safe place for chickens and small animals. Some families hewed, or trimmed flat, the sides of the logs; others left the bark in place, believing it prevented wood rot, and trimmed only the branches and twigs. To "scotch" a log was to trim the bark from the wood and was often the job of women and children.

The work inspired popular sayings still in use. As the settlers chopped and watched the wood fly, one may have pointed out how a neighbor boy resembled his father and was a "chip off the old block," recalling an English saying. If the men concerned themselves with the larger outcome of their labor and did not worry about small pieces of wood, then they "let

Log cabins in the Boonslick used a basic style of construction. A cabin could require forty logs, each twelve feet long. The logs were notched at each end and laid into place. As the walls rose higher, the builder placed two logs up against the walls as "ramps" and rolled the remaining logs up and over on top of one another. Some cabins had a sleeping loft. This was made by placing shorter, light logs across the "crib" or bottom half of the cabin, then building up the walls one or more logs high to provide headroom. The last set of logs was not trimmed to twelve feet, and so extended into the cabin. This is where posts were set to hold the roof's center pole, or ridgepole. Smaller poles called purlins ran from short end to short end of the cabin and held the roof covering. The roof was constructed by laying pieces of bark or long, thinner slices of wood called "clapboards" or "shakes" (we know them as shingles) over the purlins. The clapboards were held in place by poles tied to the purlins with rope or vines. (From *Centennial History of Missouri*, by Walter B. Stevens, State Historical Society of Missouri, Columbia)

the chips fall where they may." This phrase still means not worrying about the consequences if something has to be done.

Once the cabin was up, the spaces between the logs were filled with chinking and daubing. Settlers found plenty of red clay in Missouri. The clay was easily dug up, then thinned with water and packed between the gaps. The mud was sometimes mixed with horsehair or pig bristles to give it body for packing. One Howard County cabin built in 1816 had pieces of walnut wood angled into the spaces between the logs. These formed a framework on which to slather the clay and mud, and resulted in firm chinking. Cabins were not always pretty, but they were home. One cabin from the territory years was described as having:

> its corners projecting and hung with horse collars, gears, rough towels, dish cleaners and calabashes! it had moreover a very rude puncheon floor, a clapboard roof, and a clapboard door; while for a window a log in the erection had been skipped, and through this longitudinal aperture came light and—also wind, it being occasionally shut at first with a blanket, afterwards with a clapboard shutter. Neither nail nor spike held any part of the cabin together; and even the door was hung not with iron, but with broad hinges of tough bacon skin.

(A calabash was a squash or gourd.)

Once a cabin "crib," or room, was completed, the fireplace, chimney opening, and windows were cut out of the logs. Glass was expensive or not available, so windows were covered with wooden shutters or animal hides. If the builder had heavy paper on hand, he coated it with animal fat, making the paper translucent. Once tacked across the window opening, the paper allowed some light to enter the cabin and kept out some of the wind. The chimney itself was built up on the outside of the cabin. A framework of sticks and stones was constructed, and then the structure was covered with a mixture of thick mud and straw. Sometimes stones were placed into the chimney to act as a heat shield, and the mud helped to stop the chimney's logs from burning, but fire was always a problem on the frontier. (Reportedly, at least one cabin was saved by using the contents of a chamber pot to douse the flames!)

Building a chimney took skill: the angle of the chimney stack, the chimney height, and the size of the fireplace opening all affected how much heat remained inside the cabin. As the air heated and rose up the chimney to the cold outside, a "draft" or pull of air was created. If the draft was weak, the smoke remained inside the house and made folks' eyes water. A badly constructed chimney would actually pull the warm air outside. Olive Boone, a daughter-in-law of Daniel Boone, was a skilled chimney builder, as her husband, Nathan Boone, told a visitor around 1805:

> My wife, Olive, had a loom but no convenient place to put it, so she took possession of the deserted shop while my father and I were away hunting. The weather was cold, and there was no fireplace in the old

shop; the Negro girl was sent to the nearest neighbor a mile off to obtain the loan of a crosscut saw, with which Olive and the girl cut through several courses of logs until a suitable-sized aperture for a fireplace was made. Then with stones for the fireplace, sticks for the chimney, and mud for mortar these lone women erected a chimney, the draft of which proved decidedly the best of any on the farm.

The fireplace was for cooking as well as warmth, with a stone or even a bare earth floor serving as the hearth. The chimney took some of the smoke and smells from the cabin, but they also took the heat. A woman could stand only inches away from a fireplace and her boiling pots and feel no heat. There was little that was comfortable about a Missouri winter spent in a Boonslick cabin, and settlers arrived year round. One Arrow Rock man built his family home in January, a few years before the Santa Fe Trail opened. The weather had turned brutally cold, and the frozen ground made it impossible to mix the mud for daubing and chinking the cabin. Not to be discouraged, the settler built a fire in the middle of his cabin floor, and as the ground thawed, he mixed the chinking and daubed the mud between the logs from inside the cabin.

Chimney smoke served other purposes as well: a farmer or hunter would stand outside and watch to see if the smoke from a chimney rose up into the sky or flattened close to the cabin, a way to predict the weather. If the smoke went straight up, it would be a fine day; if the smoke hugged the cabin, then rain was in the forecast.

Cabins provided protection from weather and some privacy, although families often had to make do with a single room and a loft. Modesty was difficult to maintain: the men would turn their backs when the women were getting dressed or go outside and wait their turn. It was difficult to keep a secret in a cabin filled with grandparents, parents, and children. Sometimes, a settler might "lock" his door by using a latchstring. The latchstring was attached to the inside latch or lock of the door. A hole was drilled above the latch, and the string put through it and to the outside. When the latchstring was out, the family was home to visitors; when it was drawn in, it was a sign that visitors were discouraged. But even a well-built cabin could not always provide protection against intruders. Sarshall Cooper, an early Boonslick settler, was at home with his family in Cooper's Fort one stormy night. He suddenly fell dead from his chair, shot through the chest. Reportedly he was killed by an Indian who had carefully chipped through the chinking and daubing as the storm raged, covering any sounds, then had fired his rifle at Cooper through the hole. An attacker might also throw or shoot a blazing stick onto the roof in order to start a fire.

The interior of a small cabin could barely hold a family, so furniture was scarce and simple. There might be a rare piece of "boughten" furniture carried carefully from back East. Beds were built into a corner, with the walls supporting two sides of the frame. These served several people, or visitors, while others slept in the loft. A wooden table provided space for food preparation and eating, and a bench or two offered seating space. Looms and spinning wheels were as important as furniture and were given an important place in the cabin or in a separate building. Women who spun the yarn and thread for clothing were called "spinsters," a word that came to be used to describe unmarried women who stayed at home and worked for the family.

Backwoods homes were most often primitive. A traveler in the 1820s stopped at a cabin south of the Missouri River. The cabin was undaubed and the wind blew freely and fiercely through the chinks. The large family made him welcome, but the traveler was puzzled since there were no beds in sight. When the time came to turn in, the man of the house pulled up two pieces of the floor, and the family climbed down into a cellar hole lined with grass and leaves. They spent a warm night away from the winds, while the visitor shivered on the floor above.

Regardless of what a home looked like, most lacked wells, and settlers drew their water from the muddy Missouri River or a nearby spring or stream for drinking, cooking, and cleaning. Franklin had a town well that served the settlement for several years. Wells located in the river bottoms were shallow, however, only a few feet deep, and both wells and streams were often polluted by runoff from animal pens and the household privy or outhouse. Diseases such as dysentery, cholera, fevers, and the "summer complaint" (diarrhea) caused much misery and many deaths. People often preferred rum, whiskey, or hard cider to water. In fact, cider contained vitamins which prevented scurvy and other diseases, an improvement over a mug of thick river water.

Missouri women experienced Indian attacks, cholera epidemics, house fires, and river floods, but many survived the challenges and did so with a sense of accomplishment and grace. Nothing about frontier life was simple. Just getting to the region took weeks, bumping in a wagon or walking alongside the horses and cow when the road was muddy or flooded. Hannah Cole, cousin to Daniel Boone through marriage, traveled by wagon, horse, and pirogue (dugout canoe) to get to her new home. Mary Wetmore's journey from New York to Missouri took several months, filled with adventure. She traveled by keelboat with her husband and children, one of whom fell overboard and had to be rescued by a sailor. Another tragedy was prevented when a servant used Mary's hatboxes to buoy himself up and float over to a drowning girl.

Once in Missouri, Mary divided her households between Franklin and St. Louis, where her husband, Alphonso, was posted as paymaster for the military. At least one of her homes was a log cabin, and in it she raised eight children on the frontier. Alphonso described his family's journey up river as well as overland. He knew the Cole family from Loutre Island, and his description of his trip reflects the earlier travels of Hannah Cole and family. "I took the *divide* through Grand Prairie, and made the first track where the old St. Charles road ran, to the crossing of Bonne Femme, where New Franklin now is. Ten or twelve miles on, I halted in a prairie-bottom, opposite Arrow Rock, and made a crop." "Making a crop" meant planting corn—a house might wait, but a family's food could not.

Cooking was done in the fireplace by suspending pots and pans from chains or placing them on the coals. A housewife could mix corn cake dough in a pot, place the cakes in the embers, then turn the pot over to form an "oven" above the baking cakes. Once the cakes were finished, the cook took them out of the coals and dusted the ash off with a turkey feather. Dinner was the main meal of the day and served at noon. Supper came at the end of the day and was simple, perhaps a slab of corn pone with buttermilk. Settlers could purchase fine white flour in the town of Franklin, but some preferred the heartier taste of corn, which was easily raised in the long Boonslick summers.

Santa Te traders left in the spring and returned before winter if all went as planned. This allowed them to take out loans and mortgages and repay them before the end of the year, when they came due. But their absence meant that the wives had to manage the growing and harvesting of crops such as corn, watermelons, and beans. Corn was such an important crop that even during the War of 1812, when the Franklin area was under threat of attack, slaves and women worked the cornfields while armed men patrolled the land.

Sarah Rella Dunlop, a citizen of Franklin, wrote to the *American Farmer* magazine in 1821 to boast of the local crops. She commented on plums, gooseberries, mint, millet, honey locust, coffee nut, and corn. The latter included Mandan corn (named for the Mandan tribe of the upper Missouri River), stock corn, broom corn, and chocolate corn. Mandan corn, according to Sarah, ripened early and was planted in gardens. The troops upriver at Council Bluffs gathered more than 120 bushels of Mandan corn per acre. Stock corn was fed to the cattle, and broom corn was used to make sweeping brooms. Sarah was most proud of the chocolate corn, which had dark brown kernels. She noted that "it was used by the first settlers . . . instead of Chocolate and is a good substitute . . . [It] might very well be introduced in the manufacturing of chocolate and be a saving of much expense in the purchase of cocoa nuts."

Corn was brewed into a potent liquor that livened many a Fourth of July celebration. Cornmeal was made into porridge and baked into cakes. These cakes had lively names: pone (from an Indian word, *apone*), donnicks (perhaps from *doughnuts*), hoe cakes (the cakes were baked on the back of a flat farm implement), Johnny or journey cakes (they were baked and taken along with travelers), and dodgers (it is unclear why "dodging" or avoiding something was associated with corncakes!). Whatever the name, the cakes were baked in the coals, dusted off with a turkey feather, and served with buttermilk or butter. Another common corn dish was hominy. To make this, corn kernels were soaked in wood ash lye until the tough hull slipped off. The grain was then dried and ground into meal. Backwoods families sometimes used a simple mill called a hominy block. The block consisted of a hollowed-out log standing on end. The log was set under a sapling that was pulled down and tied to a heavy wood beater so that the young tree acted like a spring. The corn was put into the log and then the beater was bounced up and down to grind the corn. Travelers said you could find a backwoods settlement by listening for the thumping of a hominy block. Franklin farmers were fortunate to have a horse-powered gristmill, a large investment for any frontier town. The millstones were shipped from St. Louis and had to be sharpened or "dressed" to keep the mill running smoothly. Stone-ground cornmeal was the most common grain product, but along with the corn, the millwheels also ground in tiny bits of stone. This resulted in a common health problem—bad teeth—since folks wore down their teeth on the meal. But cornbread remained a popular dish, quick and simple to bake, satisfying when drenched in honey, and with a taste that brought back memories of home. In 1846, Santa Fe trader Romulus Culver wrote plaintively from the trail to his wife Mary, "If I could only get a glass of butter milk and a corn cake I would get along well enough."

Cooks could choose from a variety of meats, including pork (hogs fed on acorns in the woods), chickens, and wild game such as deer, squirrels, elk, bear, and possum. Turkeys, waterfowl, and partridge were also plentiful. Samuel Cole, who grew up in the Boonslick, boasted of shooting twenty-two bears in three days and four elk in an hour. He recalled deer were so unused to humans that all he had to do was hold up a red cloth; the deer were attracted to it out of curiosity and ambled into shooting range. Wild plants provided greens that were boiled with fat; the bitter greens were thought to thin out the blood after a winter of heavy foods. Crops raised in the Boonslick included turnips, cucumbers, cabbages, melons, snap beans, corn, cymlins (or squash), and watermelons. In 1823, the estate of one George Christman was listed as owning three fields of corn, wheat in stacks, potatoes, garden vegetables, sheep, hogs, geese, horses, and cattle.

Cows provided milk, butter, and buttermilk. Leaves from plants such as the "spice-bush" were gathered and brewed into a beverage that substituted for tea. Summer brought wild berries while fruits and nuts were gathered in the fall. Sweetening was provided by boiling down the sap of maple trees into syrup or by finding a bee tree and gathering honey. Both sugar and salt were important for preserving foods. Samuel Cole was famous for his ability to find a honey tree. He knew that bees stopped working when it was cold, so searching for honey had to be done on a warm day. He taught others to look under trees for "bee bread," a section of the honeycomb and dead bees. Honeybees, called "white man's flies" by the Indians because they arrived with the white settlers, thrived on the wildflowers and prairie grasses. Cole told of finding trees filled with forty pounds and more of clear honey—on one trip, he located more than thirteen honey trees within a small area of forest. Although finding, raising, and preparing food was time-consuming, people in the Boonslick ate well.

There were few doctors along the Missouri Trail, and getting a doctor to a sickbed could take hours or even days. Instead of depending upon medical professionals, women cared for their families with homemade remedies. Boonslick women warmed sheep's wool and tucked it in a patient's ear to soothe an ache. They treated infections with animal lard or raw meat laid on in order to reduce the swelling and draw out the heat, and gathered mustard seed to be mashed and made into a "plaster." The natural heat generated by the chemicals in the plant burned out any pain or ache. The wasp known as a "dirt dauber" built nests of fine mud; if the dried nest was crushed, the dust made a good substitute for powder to stop skin rashes. Corn whiskey and honey were mixed and swallowed in order to treat a cough. Stomach problems were settled with brews of natural ingredients such as sumac bark, snakeroot, and pine gum soaked in liquor. Wild plants were boiled into teas to settle stomachs made queasy by bad meat or sour milk.

Those families with cash to spend could purchase many different "patent" medicines. In his play *The Pedlar,* which was set in Franklin, Alphonso Wetmore lampooned the medicines: "One case of family medicines, [consisted] of Doctor Rodgers' vegetable pulmoniac detirgent decoction, Lee's Scotch ointment, Relf's cough drops, Lee's patent Windham bilious pills (warranted not to stick in the throat), Redheiffer's patent cathartic perpetual motion and so on." Since most of these medicines were made with corn whiskey and herbs, the patient who drank a bottle probably soon did not care how he felt.

Sanitation was not simple in Missouri trail towns. The only refrigeration was provided by nature. Housewives wrapped meat and butter in heavy paper and let the food soak in a cool spring or well. Meat that was "high," or somewhat rotten, had been food for flies, which deposited larvae that hatched maggots. Hunger was a good sauce, indeed, and a busy housewife would scrape off the insects and cook up the meat. Fruits were dried in the sun or cut up and strung on thread. Flies and wasps were not chased away, since it was believed the insects sucked out the juices and helped the fruit dry more quickly. Few people washed their hands or used hot water to clean food utensils so it is not surprising that Boonslick women cared for many stomach complaints. Summer cholera was a common ailment, causing stomach cramps, nausea, and many trips to the chamber pot or outhouse.

The unrelated and deadly Asiatic cholera arrived in the Boonslick by the 1830s. The disease was caused by an easily transmitted bacteria that thrived in crowded conditions, like those on a steamboat or in a city or town. One trail traveler wrote in 1849 from St. Louis, "We staid 4 or 5 days in St. Louis making preparations for our journey but left as soon as possible on account of the Cholera . . . as the Boats land from [New Orleans] you see the Hearse drive down to take off the dead . . . A young man . . . took sick in the morning and died about 5 O.C. and we buried him on the bank of the river by torch light . . . on a lonely spot." Little could be done to treat Asiatic cholera, whose victims often died quickly of dehydration, but desperate people tried various remedies to ward off the disease. They burned kettles of sulphur on street corners and fired shotguns in order to "clear" the air. One minister warned his flock to pray, trust in the Lord, and avoid green apples. Unripened fruit was thought to be unhealthy and cause severe intestinal discomfort.

But the most common disease suffered in Missouri river towns was the *ague,* malaria. The bite of an infected mosquito transmitted the disease, and the sufferer could be doomed to a lifetime of severe bouts of chills and fevers. Some people died of ague (pronounced a-gew), but many endured and learned to predict an attack. One Audrain County pioneer recalled, "A man would be plowing and at the end of the row he would lie down and have his chill, and then get up and work again. After the first chill the 7th, 14th and 21st were the days of probable recurrence, and a man would make no serious engagements on those days." To treat the ague, the soft inner bark of the slippery elm tree was made into a jelly, then mixed with bitter quinine. This was more easily swallowed by a patient suffering chills and fever. Victims of malaria were also treated with quinine bark dissolved in wine, and then followed up with cathartic pills. The pills caused stomach cramps intended to clear out the patient's bowels. This was thought to help cleanse the body of disease. Not until Dr. John Sappington developed his malaria pills, in 1832, could a mother rest easier when her children had a fever.

Early Franklin was a raw frontier community. Streets turned from dust to deep slippery mud after a rain. Horse and pig manure were raked up from the streets and walkways only after the droppings became a nuisance to walk through. Hogs rooted for food in the streets. Horses wandered the town until they were "taken up" by a neighbor and the owner notified in the newspaper. Chickens scraped for insects on the manure

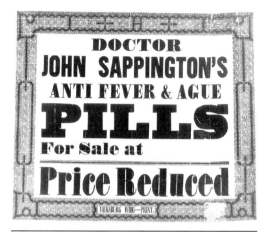

John Sappingon, who emigrated from Tennessee to the Boonslick in 1819, was the first doctor to discover a method for preventing the terrible fevers and shakes of malaria. His pills included quinine and flavoring—they were inexpensive to purchase and easy to swallow, a vast improvement over earlier malaria treatments. In later years William Becknell sold the pills to travelers. (Handbill in the Western Historical Manuscript Collection, University of Missouri in Columbia.)

piles or dunghills. Some people said dunghill chickens produced the best-tasting eggs.

The Boonslick was the edge of the Far West, but the town of Franklin was surprisingly well supplied with manufactured "boughten" goods, even in its early days. By 1821, women could purchase fine food, cloth, and clothing from several Franklin general stores owned by Misters Lamme, Tiffany, Stanley, and Ludlow as well as other merchants. Among items listed in 1821 advertisements were fashionable hats, Mackinaw blankets, morocco leather shoes, and fabric such as tartan plaids, calicoes, dimities, nankeens, and ginghams. Specialty shops stocked perfumes and cigars, pound cake, silk handkerchiefs, books, and writing papers and implements. The advertisements also contained announcements for kerseys (a coarse woolen cloth) and nailed shoes. These rough clothes were for the slaves.

But the lack of hard money and the poor economy meant some people could not purchase goods and had to rely on their own skills for daily needs. The missionary John Peck described a family he visited in 1820 only a few miles from "Booneville":

> It was not from destitution of water that the whole family remained unwashed, for a fine spring burst out within twenty yards of the cabin. Their dress was an object that attracted my attention. . . . Not a particle of *cloth* of any kind did I discover about their bodies. Men and women were dressed in skins that once the wild deer claimed, but covered and saturated with blood, grease, and dirt.

Deerskin was easy to work into clothing—at least, easier than raising, preparing, spinning, and weaving cloth. The hunter shot and skinned the animal, then treated the hide so it would be supple and comfortable to wear. For this, Indians buried the hides in the earth several days and then removed the hair. The hide was then scraped clean, soaked, stretched, and smoked. Once treated in this way, the hide remained soft and easy to cut and lace into clothing. The edges were sometimes cut into fringe, which was more than decorative: fringe channeled rain to run off the deerskin and its swinging movement kept away insects.

Alphonso Wetmore depicted many aspects of Boonslick life in his play *The Pedlar*. Written in 1821, *The Pedlar* has a backwoods character called Opposum, who boasts how easy it was to create a "suit" of clothes from deerskin: "What do you think this suit cost me? I'll tell you, one charge of rifle powder, half an ounce of lead, four pence ha'penny worth of allum water, and two hours labor." Allum (alum) was a mineral used in the tanning process. It drew water from the "green" or fresh skin and kept the skin from spoiling. Wetmore was exaggerating with "two hours," but Missouri Trail families found deerskin a practical clothing item.

The early settlement years of the Boonslick were "foothold" times, when folks were establishing their farms. Crops like cotton, which took a lot of care, had to wait a generation before becoming agricultural staples. Sheep were uncommon until the 1830s, when farms were firmly established and the animals were less likely to be victims of predators. The earliest settlers to Franklin and Boonville lacked the ability to manufacture cotton, linen, or wool cloth, so they purchased it in town. One visitor to the region commented on the plainness of the women's dresses:

This pioneer family is off to church or a social event. The mother carries her shoes and wears a long bonnet that protects her shoulders from the sun. Father has a coonskin cap and fringed hunting frock with worn pants, and the son is wearing a long shirt. A fearsome dog accompanies them. (State Historical Society of Missouri, Columbia)

It might amuse and probably frighten, the fashionable ladies of Philadelphia, to witness a gathering of the softer sex on the frontier. Their uniform dress is a gown of coarse cotton, usually called here "factory cloth" or "gingham." It is covered with very narrow stripes, or sometimes check. The head gear is a bonnet of the same stuff, in the form that in the old States is called a sun bonnet. This is worn through the day, in the house or out of it, especially when company is present.

When store-bought fabric was too expensive or buckskin would not do, women turned to the Missouri River bottoms. There, acres of nettles grew, and the pioneers knew how to turn the plants into shirts, trousers, and petticoats. Wild nettle plants produce long, tough fibers strong enough for spinning and weaving. In early spring, Boonslick women gathered nettles that had rotted over the winter. Nettles were prickly plants with a natural chemical that caused itching and rashes, but by leaving the nettles to rot before collecting them, the women avoided the discomfort. The plants were then beaten or "broke" until the fibers separated, after which the women could spin threads and, finally, weave the cloth. The thread produced a soft fabric, and the roots could be boiled to produce a yellow dye.

Men's trail clothing was little different in town. Depending upon the man, it could be as simple as jeans trousers with a shirt and vest, or it could reflect the character of the wearer. Reverend Nicholas Patterson wrote in 1818 of one man near Franklin.

> I met a man the other day about forty years of age, in the woods, whom I found, in conversation, to be a *preacher,* and afterwards I learned he was much beloved and respected by his neighbors . . . his outside garment was a *hunting shirt,* so called, a kind of loose, open frock, with large sleeves, the body open in front, lapped over and belted with a leather girdle and buckle. The cape, or shoulder piece, was large, and fringed. Its material was dressed deer skin, of a yellowish cast. His vest and pants were made of cloth, a mixture of wool and cotton, of a light blue color. He wore leggings of dressed skin, and a pair of moccasins in place of boots. He carried a rifle on his shoulder, and had his shot pouch and accoutrements for hunting, including a large knife, stuck in his belt. For a covering to the head he wore a sort of cap made of a wolf's skin, with the hair on, and the tail fastened up behind. His beard was black, and the growth of a week.

Certainly Reverend Patterson must have looked very dull next to his colorfully clad backwoods brother.

Slavery played a large role in Missouri's Boonslick settlement and in Santa Fe Trail history, although much of its story remains to be told. Henry M. Brackenridge reported in 1811 that Braxton Cooper was then managing the salt works and a settlement was located nearby. "They are generally persons in good circumstances, most of them own slaves." The Missouri Compromise of 1820 banned slavery outside the proposed state of Missouri but allowed the institution within Missouri's boundaries. In writing the Compromise, Congress thought it less inflammatory to say where slavery was not allowed, rather than to say where it was allowed: "That in all that territory ceded by France to the United States, under the name of Louisiana, which lies north of thirty-six degrees and thirty minutes north latitude, not included within the limits of the state . . . slavery and involuntary servitude, . . . shall be, and is hereby, forever prohibited."

Many Boonslick settlers had come from Southern states including Virginia, Kentucky, North Carolina, and Tennessee, where slavery was part of life. When the families emigrated to the Missouri territory, they brought their slaves with them. Hannah Cole and her trader sons owned the slaves Isaac and Lucy. Whether Isaac and Lucy were married is not known. Miles Meredith Marmaduke, a Franklin trader and later governor of Missouri, wrote to his friend John Hardeman from Taos, New Mexico, asking Hardeman to take care of his slaves and not abuse them, to have the slaves avoid "violent cold," and to hire them out for work. Marmaduke took two slaves with him on an 1824 trip to Santa Fe. Some traders had neighbors and friends manage their slaves while they were gone to Mexico.

When the Missouri traders went to Santa Fe, many left their families behind to cope as best they could with the help of slaves. Becknell's wife Mary managed their land and faced down creditors suing her husband for debt. Alphonso Wetmore's wife Mary had been raised on the Mohawk Valley frontier in New York State, but nothing prepared her for raising several children (including a newborn), managing a farm, and feeding and clothing family and slaves for the year her husband was gone to New Mexico. She, like many other women, depended upon slaves. When Wetmore was not able to pay some debts, the slaves were removed from the family and threatened with being sold downriver to the cotton plantations of Louisiana, but he managed to have his debts paid and the slaves returned. Military officer and trader Wetmore considered himself a respected master, commenting on his return from a trip to Baltimore in 1824 that

> I found my wife & children in excellent health; and every member of my family, including the blacks and my spaniel dog, were exceedingly glad to see me again among them. This classification of my negroes and dog together may appear a little unchristian; but when it is remembered the former poor divils have generally . . . a dogs life of it, it may not be esteemed mal apropos.

Dog's life or not, Wetmore, as far as is known, did not free his slaves during his lifetime.

Franklin limited the rights of slaves to assemble in groups, and patrollers made certain the slaves were not out at night. Notices in the Boonslick newspaper for the capture of runaway slaves illustrate the many desperate attempts of enslaved men and women to gain freedom. One 1821 advertisement in the *Missouri Intelligencer and Boonslick Advertiser* showed how little the slave owner knew about his "property," including the date of the child's birth: "For sale—A likely Negro boy, about 15 years of age." Another notice, by James Hickman, suggested the value owners placed on slaves.

> Stop the Runaway! $25 Reward. Ran away from the subscriber in Franklin Missouri on the 6th. . a NEGRO MAN named JIM, about 35 years old, about 5 feet 8 or 10 inches high, very black and tolerable large eyes . . . slow spoken and with a down look. Had on when he went away a wool hat, pretty well worn, a white roundabout coat of twilled linsey, tow linen pantaloons; white woolen socks, new shoes, pegged in the bottom. The above reward will be given to any person who will deliver said negro to James Hickman, in Franklin, or confine him in some jail so that the subscriber gets him again, and all reasonable charges paid. (Nov. 11, 1825.)

Some slaves fought against their fate, with terrible consequences: in 1826, Luke Harris was hanged in Boonville for killing his owner. Slaves were purchased and leased out to other farmers who wanted to raise labor-intensive crops like hemp and tobacco. The man who leased slaves also paid for their food and clothing; sometimes the slaves were paid a little as well, but most often spent lives of unremitting labor and hardship.

When the Santa Fe trade was beginning in Missouri, slaves accounted for nearly a quarter of the Boonslick population. Slave owners were responsible for food, clothing, housing, health, and training of the slaves. The independence offered by a successful Santa Fe trade business must have looked tempting to men who wanted slaves to keep a farm producing or a mill grinding. Many slaves became skilled artisans if given the chance to learn. Small as the settlement was, the streets of Arrow Rock were lined with deep limestone gutters that carried away heavy rains from the streets. The gutters, cut and fitted into place by slaves, are still in place, bearing witness to the care with which they were constructed. Of course, the stoneworkers' names are unknown. For the slaves, the "down look" of a runaway was easily explained.

Shape notes were a method of notation invented to help people read music. This tune, from the *Missouri Harmony,* was a popular one during the Santa Fe Trail era and reflected both a religious aspect of life as well as a desire of Americans to emigrate west. (State Historical Society of Missouri, Columbia)

Boonslick settlers enjoyed social functions year round, but the times before planting and after harvest were the most popular for cabin parties. Dances took place at the taverns and hotels, and people rode miles on horse or wagon to attend. One of Hannah Cole's sons recalled years later that as a young boy, he wanted to attend a dance upriver. Hannah Cole refused because Samuel did not have any trousers—only a long linen shirt—and she did not want him to be embarrassed at his backwoods attire. But Samuel sneaked out anyway and rode his tame bull to the dance. After he watched the entertainment, he and the bull waded into the river and Samuel held onto its tail as they swam back home.

Music was made on fiddles and drums, later on banjos and guitars. If no musical instruments were to be had, then folks sang the tunes, banged on pots and pans and stamped their feet in time to the singing, but seemingly most frolics included musicians. For folks who wanted to learn music, singing schools provided the chance. Singing schools were held in Missouri as early as the 1820s, generally after the harvest was in. A singing master came to a town, announced the school and signed up members.

The "master" was often a man who had attended a school somewhere else and traveled about making some extra silver. The schools were more like choir practice than formal training. Students brought their own candles and purchased a shape note songbook, such as *The Missouri Harmony*, published in 1820. Songs were printed with shapes—a diamond, square, circle, and triangle—that indicated intervals between notes. Women and men attended nightly classes for several weeks, reading the music by candlelight and learning to read the "shapes" of notes and associate them with sounds.

Many hymns echoed the lives of western emigrants: the song "Canaan" had a verse that declared "I am bound for the promised land," much as the emigrants were bound for western settlements. In "Amanda," people sang "Death, like an overflowing stream, Sweeps us away, our life's a dream," familiar thoughts for those who watched cholera and dysentery kill friends and neighbors. But despite some dark lyrics, shape note singing was a loud and vibrant style of music that came west with the emigrants. That Santa Fe traders were familiar with it is shown in a story by Alphonso Wetmore. In the tale, a New Englander visiting the frontier and out on the trail is attacked by a bear. Instead of turning to run, the man began to sing loudly and beat out a shape note tune, sending the bear into a terrified retreat.

Missouri was known for the irreligious and wild ways of the frontiersmen. "The boast was often made that the Sabbath never had crossed and never should cross the Mississippi," reported Reverend John Peck, an observation attributed to Timothy Flint. Reverend Peck reported on the oddities and ways of this new western world. One often-told story was about Judge Tucker, who reportedly lived in a log cabin and had his law office in a hollowed out sycamore tree. Another time Peck enjoyed an afternoon with Daniel Boone at the frontiersman's home near St. Charles. But Peck was not happy with what he found in the Boonslick. The region was known for its boisterous nature and many fights. He was shocked by people who did not read the Bible, went on "sprees," drank liquor, and played cards. Some thought the fiddle was the Devil's instrument because it encouraged dancing and other questionable behavior. But most considered the fiddle a way to share good times with friends. As early as 1820, the merchant Jacob Wyan of Boonville noted in his ledger book that he had a fiddle and strings for sale. Wyan was so lonesome for the sound, he paid one of his customers to play the fiddle, and then gave him some whitewash for his house as a bonus.

Muster Day for the militia occurred three times a year, when all able-bodied men gathered to drill and practice military maneuvers. All male inhabitants between the ages of sixteen and sixty served in their local military districts. The day quickly became a time to picnic with friends and enjoy apples, gingerbread, and whiskey or hard cider. An even more potent beverage could be made by letting hard cider freeze—the liquid that remained unfrozen was "farmer's applejack," which had a stronger kick than any Missouri mule. Temperance may have been preached by ministers ("Adam's ale" was water), but from an economic and practical point of view, alcohol ruled frontier life. On Muster Days, Santa Fe traders like Benjamin Cooper and Stephen Cole participated in the fun, which generally ended up with a number of fights between rival groups and communities.

People shared work and play at corn shuckings (stripping the corn of its husk), quiltings, log rollings (chopping and trimming trees), house raisings, and plain fun "frolicks." Dinners in commemoration of special events were also popular. In 1819, Franklin celebrated the arrival of the *Independence,* the first steamboat to reach the town. Many toasts were called for, and speakers offered "regular" or invited toasts and "volunteer" or unscheduled toasts. Among the toasts in Franklin were *"The Missouri River,* its last wave will roll the abundant tribute of our region to the Mexican gulf," oddly predicting the opening of the Santa Fe Trail.

April 1821 saw a public dinner at Captain Means' hotel in Franklin to celebrate Missouri's defeat of Eastern politicians who wanted to manipulate the Missouri government. "We enjoy the right of self-government . . . and it was with this view the dinner was given," the *Missouri Intelligencer and Boonslick Advertiser* announced. After dinner, toasts were offered in honor of Missouri, Congress, the Constitution, farmers, and the local fair. Future Santa Fe traders Augustus Storrs and William Becknell raised their glasses in honor of the new state and the new governor. Washington's birthday was celebrated in the Boonslick with dances and barbecues including honey doughnuts, possum and sweet potatoes, "flour doins" (baked goods), wine, and whiskey. Two hotels vied to outdo each other in entertainment. Musicians were hired, including fiddlers and tambourine and triangle players. The ladies dressed in gowns and fancy shoes and wore red or green ribbons for their favorite sponsor. They even curled their hair and displayed as much finery or "crinkum crankum" as they owned.

But the favorite holiday of all Boonslickers was Independence Day. The United States was young in 1821, and some elderly Franklin men still recalled the American Revolution. A typical celebration described by Alphonso Wetmore took place in Franklin in the late 1820s. The day's events—called a "jubilee"—began with the firing of a small cannon in rivalry with Boonville (and the Coopers). The booms were so loud they "went windin along the hills till they get tired of this yearth and then go clean to heaven" as one citizen claimed. After that fun was over, the young men of the town went hunting and brought back meat for a "berbacue" at the local spring and picnic ground. Soup was set over the fire to cook and when done, it was passed around with a little whiskey in it to "correct the heat." The brown jug of whiskey was shared through the meal, and then "orations" began. At one point, the main speaker stripped down to his unmentionables, climbed into a tree, began an oration, and then, overcome by the "spirit in the bottle," fell gracefully to earth. Across the river in Boonville, festivities began when a new cannon was fired from the top of an Indian mound on High Street, above the Missouri River. Then residents enjoyed a picnic and a public reading of the Declaration of Independence near the courthouse and finally dances, games, and gossip.

One popular entertainment was practical jokes, many of which were rough and cruel. Men put too much gunpowder in someone's weapon to see how the victim would handle the kick when the gun was fired. Alphonso Wetmore took part in a "prank" where Army soldiers threatened to shoot a man as a traitor (the poor fellow had tried to protect his crops from being raided by the military). A drunken soldier was hauled up before a mock court one Muster Day and accused, falsely, of trying to kill people. The judge threatened to hang the man, who was then "warned" by his "defense attorney" (one of the jokers) to make a break for it. The man jumped out the window, leaped on a horse, and never, folks said, returned to Boonville. Mark Cole, son of Santa Fe trader Stephen Cole, decided to hide one night near a new grave and scare young ladies walking home. Graves in those days were covered with wooden frames and "roofs" in order to keep animals away. When Mark sat down on the grave to wait, it began to shift and move, and howling came from beneath the ground. Mark didn't wait to find out what it was—he ran for home, only

FEAT OF MIKE FINK.

Mike Fink was the most famous boatman on the western rivers. Known for his strength, shooting feats, and practical jokes, Fink may have visited Franklin, Missouri, during one of his upriver trips. Here, he is shown shooting a cup from the head of very trusting friend. According to legend, Fink eventually missed a shot, killed a man, and was later shot himself. (State Historical Society of Missouri, Columbia)

to discover later that his "friends" had discovered his plans and decided to turn the tables on him. Mark would never travel alone at night after that.

In Missouri, and especially in the settlements, fighting was as common as the ague and a great deal more fun—at least from fighters' points of view. A man might sue a neighbor for a perceived wrong or be fined for causing problems in town. But sometimes it was just as easy to try to settle problems with a fight, especially for someone who had been enjoying a jug of whiskey at the tavern. Like frontier life in Missouri, fights were rough and tumble, hard and nasty. Court documents contain descriptions of fights in the early days of the Boonslick. In 1819, the Hicklin brothers, John and Barnett, pulled Mary Turner out of her house for an unknown reason and "plucked . . . large quantities of her hair . . . off her head . . . and with stick and their fists struck" her. The defendants were hauled into court for slapping, punching, kicking, and beating Mary.

Stanley Morgan, who helped his father Asa lay out the new town of Boonville, was a skilled bully. Although he was always fined five dollars for assault and battery, he was brought into court again and again for the same crime. In 1821, four ruffians attacked a warmly dressed Alexander Allen and tore off his clothes, including "one great coat, one other coat, two waist coats, one shirt, two pair of breeches and one hat." Poor Mr. Allen was then thrown about in the snow. A notice printed in 1822 announced that William Turner tried to kill W. H. Curtis. Turner was fined $500 and sentenced to a year in the Boonville jail. But in December, he broke out and headed south. People were warned he was small, blond, and "subject to drink, quarrelsome and abusive in his language."

Despite their spirits and fists, the Boonville boys couldn't hold a candle to the most famous brawler in America, Mike Fink. Fink was from Pittsburgh. Famous as a keelboatman on the Mississippi and Ohio rivers, and later, as a fur trapper, he traveled the Missouri as far as the Yellowstone River. Folks in Franklin may have preferred to have Fink avoid their town: one of his pranks was to gather up some boatmen, stretch a rope across a street, and run full speed through town, tossing people to and fro. Fink expected people to laugh at his jokes: after all, he reasoned, he was telling them for a reason and did not want anyone to "make light of them" by remaining silent. There is no mention of Fink in the *Missouri Intelligencer,* but Alphonso Wetmore included a character based on the keelboatman in his play *The Pedlar,* and audiences recognized Fink immediately. In his later years, Fink traveled up the Missouri River and was killed during a fight. Frontier people had to be tough, willing to take anything that was dished out. It was to this world that a settler named William Becknell had come in 1812.

CHAPTER 2

"As far as we wish to go"

William Becknell Leads the Way

⸺⸰⸺

A TRAIL BRINGS PEOPLE, COMMERCE, and places together. It shows the way. It suffers from bad weather. It has a name and a character. A trail is in some ways, alive. And if necessity was the mother of the Santa Fe Trail and trade, then William Becknell was its father. Becknell was born in Virginia around 1788. Little is known of his early life, but by 1811 he had moved west of St. Louis, where he worked for a shop owner and trader near St. Charles. One day in 1812, Becknell traveled to St. Louis to deliver a gun and horse to Robert McKnight, another Virginian.

Soon after the St. Louis meeting, McKnight and several other men left on a trading trip to the Southwest. They believed Mexico was about to declare its independence from Spain and hoped to benefit as traders under a newly free and open market. But McKnight's information was wrong. In fact, the Mexican revolutionaries were defeated and executed, and instead of finding a welcome, the McKnight party was arrested by the Spanish authorities for entering the country illegally and imprisoned for nine years.

Perhaps tall, red-haired William Becknell had known of McKnight's plans. He may have thought McKnight was foolhardy or that Missouri was a better place to make a fortune. Whatever the reason, Becknell did not join the trading party but instead moved farther west and went to work at the Boones' salt lick. It was difficult work. The salty water was drawn up from a well, then poured into huge iron kettles. After the water

Missouri at statehood was an "incomplete" state. It would add counties until 1876, when St. Louis County was divided from St. Louis City. The Santa Fe Trail crossed many of the present-day mid-Missouri counties, including Howard, Cooper, Cole, Saline, and Jackson. (State Historical Society of Missouri, Columbia)

boiled away, the salt was scraped out and packed into bushels. Tree after tree was chopped into firewood to keep the kettles going from sunup to dark. Besides the work, the salt makers were harassed by Indians, who stole horses and made a rough life even more challenging. Nathan Boone, a friend of Becknell, recalled the work would have been profitable "but for the troubles and pilferings of the Indians at the works for several years, chiefly in stealing and killing the working and beef cattle."

During the War of 1812, the Boonslick region became an even more dangerous place. The British encouraged Indian attacks on the Americans, hoping to weaken their hold on the western territory. Settlers in the Boonslick region constructed several forts near present-day Boonville and north of the river near New Franklin, Petersburg, and Rocheport. Built of logs set upright, with high walls and vantage points for riflemen and defenders, the forts were to provide safe harbor to families, slaves, and livestock during attacks. Not all forts had a spring inside the walls, so obtaining water was sometimes a problem. On the Boonville side of the Missouri, the only fort in America named for a woman—Hannah Cole—stood on the Missouri bluffs. In time of attack, buckets were lowered into the river for water, which prevented the enemy from burning the fort or driving the settlers out from thirst.

William Becknell joined Daniel Morgan Boone in a cavalry company of rangers formed to protect the settlers. Each soldier provided his own clothing, food, rifle, and ammunition, and each was responsible for finding forage for his horse. Foot soldiers were paid 75¢ a day, while men who owned horses and "ranged" far afield were paid $1.00, which the soldiers did not receive until after the war. These rangers traveled from Franklin to St. Louis and into Illinois and Iowa. Becknell soon received a promotion and helped build forts near St. Charles.

After the war, Becknell returned to the Boonslick, where he boiled salt, farmed, and ran a Missouri River ferry near Arrow Rock with his brother. George Sibley, the factor, or manager, at Fort Osage, wrote of Becknell in 1825 that he was "a man of good character, great personal bravery, and by nature and habit hardy and enterprising. . . . He certainly had no knowledge of mercantile concerns and is tho' very shrewd and intelligent, very deficient in education." No matter how hard he tried, Captain William Becknell seemed at the mercy of the economic hard times. The goods and crops from the Boonslick cost more to send to market than to grow or produce. The people of the United States demanded help, and in Franklin a dinner was held in honor of legislators who had voted to relieve settlers from personal debt. But matters moved slowly in the Boonslick. Becknell tried to cover his debts by speculating in land as the troubles increased. He borrowed money in April 1821, purchased more land, and leased slaves to work the new property, which only succeeded in putting him deeper into debt. William Becknell was not the most skillful businessman in the Boonslick.

The times finally caught up with him, and Becknell was faced with repaying a loan or serving time in prison. For a man of Becknell's "good character" it was a terrible blow. A friend bailed him out of the debt, but the help was only temporary. He needed hard money and there were few ways to obtain it in Missouri. But Becknell had shown himself to be a man willing to take risks. He was well connected in the small Franklin community and aware of the comings and goings of his friends and neighbors. News of Mexico's recent attempts to sever its ties with Spain and declare independence had reached the territories, but no one knew if the uprising had been successful. Becknell remembered Robert McKnight, who had only recently been freed from a Mexican prison. But he also knew there was no direct river route to Mexico and therefore no trade competition from other countries. He heard from fur trappers who stopped in Franklin that beaver fur was bringing good money in St. Louis. He also heard that Mexico had silver mines and coin currency. Pushed by his debt, and despite the dangers, sometime in 1821 William Becknell decided to travel to Mexico in search of fortune.

On June 25, 1821, the *Missouri Intelligencer and Boonslick Advertiser* carried an advertisement signed by "Wm. Becknell." In it, Becknell announced he was organizing a three-month trip "as far as we wish to go," during which the group would trap beaver, hunt, and trade merchandise for horses and mules. Any man who joined would provide his own horse, "sufficient cloathing to keep him warm and comfortable," a rifle, and ammunition. Each group of eight men was to share an ax, pack horse, and tent. In addition, Becknell expected that "if the company consist of 30 or more men, 10 dollars a man will answer to purchase the quantity of merchandise required to trade on." Becknell was organizing a cooperative expedition to travel into the shadowlands between the U.S. and Spanish territories.

The men were to share the cost of the trading and divide the profits equally. Becknell insisted that the division of profits was not to take place until all had returned to the "north side of the Missouri river," to Franklin. If a man could not afford the goods and investment, he was encouraged to find a sponsor who would receive an equal share of benefits. Becknell offered a fair chance to all for profit with little investment of money. He had high hopes. The advertisement said that only seventy men would be allowed to sign on by the August 4 deadline for the journey, indicating that he assumed at least that many might apply. Seventy adventurers

Alexander McNair was the first governor of Missouri, and he encouraged the state's push for federal support of expanded trade with Mexico. Missouri was suffering severe financial problems, and in April 1824 McNair asked Congress for assistance to protect the new and profitable "commerce of the prairies." Although McNair did not travel to Santa Fe, he and Thomas Hart Benton understood the importance of the inland trade and worked to ensure that the trail remained open. (State Historical Society of Missouri, Columbia)

would be nearly double the size of any previous trapping trip. Becknell also made it clear that the trip would be almost military in organization and command. He would fine any man who signed up but did not make the journey, and he would have "every man . . . bound by an oath to submit to such orders and rules as the company when assembled shall think proper to enforce." Becknell was determined to create a democratic and well-organized trading company.

The first meeting of the group took place August 4, at Ezekiel Williams's settlement "five miles above Franklin" on the Missouri River. Seventeen men—far fewer than the hoped-for seventy—came that Monday to hear Becknell's plan. Perhaps the meeting was held outside under a grove of trees and a jug of whiskey passed around in friendship as the men listened to Becknell and asked Williams about his experiences west of the Missouri River. Ezekiel "Zeke" Williams was famous. He had participated in a trapping expedition on the upper Missouri for the St. Louis Fur Company in 1811 and was the only member of the expedition not killed or taken to a Santa Fe prison. He had survived a grizzly bear attack, spent a "wretched winter" with the Arapahoes, been captured by the Kansas Indians, and finally freed to travel with the Osage back to Franklin. Zeke Williams's firsthand knowledge of the land, tribes, and weather was of great importance to the other men. There is little doubt the men who met with Becknell were aware that "as far as we wish to go" might include a city that was off-limits to Americans—Santa Fe, the city of holy faith. In a town as small as Franklin, these plans could not have been a great secret—an unspoken understanding perhaps, but not a secret.

At the August 4 meeting, William Becknell was elected the captain of the group or caravan, as the men called it. The captain was responsible for the safety of the men. He chose the travel routes and held military control over the caravan, which was important if the caravan came under attack. It was also Becknell's responsibility to obtain permission from Alexander McNair, Missouri's first governor, to travel west. McNair had served in a St. Louis ranger company during the War of 1812, and it may be that Becknell knew him. The governor could not encourage illegal travel by Americans into disputed territory. The American frontier was short of troops, and McNair did not want a war with Spain. But he agreed to Becknell's plan to travel in the undisputed areas between Missouri and the New Mexico border. What Becknell did after that could not be blamed on the governor.

The next meeting was August 18, at "Mr. Shaw's in Franklin." Becknell commented to the *Missouri Intelligencer* that he believed thirty men would be sufficient for a company. He may have also thought that his earlier demands were a mite heavy-handed, for he said that "those who signed their names to the first article and did not appear on the 4th of this month, are excluded from going in this company, and excused from paying any fine." Becknell had not been as successful as he expected in recruiting men. Perhaps the cost of the trip was too much or three months away from their farms and families meant too much hardship for some. It is possible that some did not want William Becknell as leader or thought it was far too dangerous an undertaking. Whatever their reasons, Becknell ended up with only a few companions on the trail.

On Friday, September 1, 1821, a group of men turned out at "the place appointed on the eighteenth." This was the ferry near present-day Arrow Rock, a few miles from Franklin. Becknell and his brother had been the ferry masters there. How many men finally joined Becknell on that warm day? The answer is a mystery. Alphonso Wetmore, the first historian of the Santa Fe Trail, wrote in 1824 that Becknell had "left this place for the uninhabited country that lies between Missouri and the upper province of Mexico, for the purpose of hunting game and to procure wild horses" and then mentions "one or two of his party." In 1831 Wetmore wrote in a government report that "several citizens of Boonlick [sic] made a small outfit at this place and departed with the avowed purpose of visiting the settlements of New Mexico." From Becknell's diary, we know of two men, but not their names: "We sent out two hunters who killed a deer." Becknell also mentions that two lieutenants were elected, suggesting perhaps a party of a dozen or more. George Sibley, the factor from Fort Osage, may have answered the question. In a letter written in 1825 Sibley says of Becknell, "His followers were about   , in number all of the same description of persons . . ." Unfortunately, the writing is illegible regarding the size of the trail party. Only two names besides Becknell's have been linked with the first Santa Fe trading party: Braxton Cooper of Franklin, later killed in an Indian attack on the trail, and Ewing Young, named by Josiah Gregg in *Commerce of the Prairies*. The rest of the men are unknown to history.

Both Wetmore and Sibley were aware that Becknell's intention was never to just hunt and trap. Wetmore noted that Becknell's "avowed purpose" was for trade and Sibley wrote that "his [Becknell's] outfit consisted of a few hundred dollars worth of coarse cotton goods." No one had any doubt as to the reason for Becknell's journey: to be the first to trade with the newly free Mexicans. The men who headed west out of Franklin that day probably did not know they were citizens of the new state of Missouri. And Becknell left behind more than a state: he left his wife Mary and three children to fend off bankruptcy and debt as well as they could.

A pack train consisted of mules, pack saddles, and goods for trade. Packing a mule was an art: the load had to be well-balanced and tied down so the mule couldn't shake it off. Goods were unloaded from mules each night and repacked in the morning. (State Historical Society of Missouri, Columbia)

After leaving Arrow Rock, the caravan traveled for six miles and then set up camp. The next day "being warm and cloudless," the men rode thirty-five miles to the Petit Osage Plains, in modern Saline County. The land was described by a later visitor as "one of the most romantic and beautiful places in the State. The Traveler approaches the plain over a very high point of adjoining prairie; suddenly the eye catches a distant view of the Missouri on the right, and a growth of lofty timber adjoining it about two miles wide. . . . Description cannot do justice to such a varied prospect."

Becknell noted in his journal that rains and a cool and humid atmosphere made travel uncomfortable, "this being the time of equinoctial storms," the change of seasons when storms occurred more frequently. After arriving at Fort Osage, the men wrote letters home, purchased additional medicines, and "arranged such affairs as we thought necessary previous to leaving the confines of civilization." George Sibley had much knowledge of the Far West from his dealings with Indian tribes. He had traveled to the fabled Grand Saline in present-day Oklahoma in 1811, and he had also heard stories from a friend, Dr. John H. Robinson, who traveled west with explorer and military officer Zebulon Pike and knew of Santa Fe and the Rocky Mountains. Sibley may have shared this information with Becknell, warning of dangers both natural and human, and offering guidance to the river crossings and mountain passages. Unlike trading or trapping competitors who may have kept to themselves what knowledge they had of Santa Fe, Sibley had little to gain by keeping information from Becknell. Sibley's reputation as an able administrator and fair trader suggests he offered as much information as he had to give.

The group left Fort Osage and began their trek. Becknell wrote the Missouri country they crossed was "handsomely situated, being high prairie." Sometime after leaving Fort Osage, he and others were taken ill, perhaps from bad water or meat. They continued despite the stomach discomfort. The next journal entry indicates Becknell and company were in Kansas on September 22.

Once on the plains, the Missourians hunted game, including antelope, jackrabbits, and buffalo. Becknell shot and roasted a prairie dog, but thought the taste "strong and unpalatable." The group crossed the Arkansas River and named one of the small streams Hope Creek, perhaps reflecting their feelings about the journey. For several weeks, they followed the river to what is now southeastern Colorado and then turned south again along another river. Becknell later wrote of crossing sand hills, enduring long and heavy rain storms, drinking slimy and salty water. There were few sources of firewood so the men used dried buffalo chips for campfires, which, although good for roasting meat, did not produce a steady enough heat for baking bread or biscuits. Given the poor water and rough food, it is not surprising that the men suffered from continual illnesses. By October 21, they had run out of bread and salt, and the horses were exhausted and suffering from lack of good grazing. The men stopped for three days to allow the horses to rest and to "dress some skin for moccasins."

Hundreds of miles of walking destroyed boots and feet alike, but the men plodded on. The land was "rugged, wild and dreary." At one of the most grueling times of the trip, Becknell and his company spent two days pushing aside large rocks that blocked a mountain path. One horse fell to its death, but Becknell wrote nothing else about this tragedy. The loss of a horse meant that a man might have to walk or repack and double the weight on another horse. It also meant the loss of a companion on a lonely trail. The party had little choice but to continue. By November, snow and wind made traveling even more difficult, and Becknell wrote, "Our company is much discouraged; but the prospect of a near termination of our journey excites hope and redoubled exertion." The men moved through passes and across the plains to "Rock River," and on November 13 they "had the satisfaction of meeting with a party of Spanish troops." The men appeared friendly and escorted the caravan to a village, where Becknell met a French trapper who agreed to guide them to Santa Fe. Whether Becknell learned about Mexican independence before he arrived in Santa Fe is not known, but a few days later the caravan reached the settlement and the Americans were welcomed with "apparent pleasure and joy."

Becknell stayed in Santa Fe for a month. He says little about his time there, but he met with the governor, who encouraged the Americans to continue trading with Mexico. They might even, he suggested, emigrate and set up businesses. Becknell's time in Santa Fe and St. Michael, a smaller village, was spent in trading whatever goods had survived the journey. The Americans found the Mexican people and their culture strange, and appeared to have little interest in learning more about their new trading partners. Many Americans of the time were wary and dismissive of other cultures as unable to understand or appreciate democracy or Americans. Becknell thought the Mexicans "indolent and ignorant" but was impressed by their ability to raise crops in a land of little rain. Only days after Becknell's party arrived in Mexico, two other groups of traders rode in from the states. Becknell realized he had to return quickly with substantial trade goods if he was to cash in on the trade. By December, he was ready to leave for Missouri although his party decided to wait out the winter in Santa Fe.

Accompanied by "Mr. M'Laughin" and "two other men who had arrived there a few days before" Becknell left for home on December 13, 1821. Who the two men were has never been determined. They may have been trapping in the Santa Fe region and decided to join Becknell for safety. They were lucky in their decision. Becknell and his group took a more southern route home to Missouri. Perhaps Becknell had heard of this southern route from Zeke Williams or George Sibley, or he may have learned about it while in Mexico. The route avoided the mountain passes and cut a month of travel off the return trip. During the journey, the men purchased corn from a group of Kaw Indians and survived the winter's cold with the "great heat" provided by buffalo chips. George Sibley did not note whether Becknell stopped at Fort Osage on his return, but Sibley later wrote that the men returned with "specie, mules, asses and Spanish coverlids or blankets." On Tuesday, January 30, 1822, Becknell reached Franklin. The noisy mules and asses, the tired horses with their burdens, the people running out to see what the ruckus was about must have made a lively scene for all involved. "My father saw them unload when they returned," recalled Mr. H. Harris, "and when their rawhide packages of silver dollars were dumped on the sidewalk one of the men cut the thongs and the money spilled out and clinking on the stone pavement, rolled into the gutter." Becknell had succeeded beyond anyone's imagination, including, perhaps, his own.

Not long after his return to Missouri, Becknell settled several lawsuits against him and began to plan a spring journey to Santa Fe. If the silver "that spilled out" was the share agreed upon by the company, then Becknell profited well from a small investment in fabric. The "silver fever" spread quickly, and even a demure young woman named Fanny Marshall invested $60 in the trading venture. (She received $900, a fair return on her money.) In 1822, the *Missouri Intelligencer* published a New Year's address that included a proud mention of the new trade:

> What though in Eastern luxuries poor,
> We've Western dainties rare, in store.
> Can briny shad—can turbot vie
> With buff'lo tongue and venison-pie?
> We now a short excursion try
> Across the Rocky Hills so high,
> And now the stately Dons to see,
> We take a trip to Santa Fe.

William Becknell, a man from the brand new state of Missouri, was not the first trader or trapper to reach Santa Fe. But he was the first to get to the city, open it for trade, and return with something to show for all the danger. Thanks to Missouri, the Santa Fe Trail was now open for business.

Thomas Hart Benton was a rough and tumble politician who championed Missouri statehood and the development of the Santa Fe Trail. Known for his quick temper, Benton was as likely to resort to his fists as to his wit when faced with a challenge to his beliefs. (State Historical Society of Missouri, Columbia)

After William Becknell, it was Thomas Hart Benton who, newly elected as one of Missouri's first two U.S. senators, most quickly realized the trail's importance to Missouri. Born in North Carolina in 1782, Benton had studied law, served as a state senator in Tennessee, and helped his mother run a 2,000-acre farm. He was handsome, witty, believed in American expansion, and had a hair-trigger temper that led to a number of duels and arguments.

During the War of 1812, Benton had risen to the rank of colonel and served as first aide to General Andrew Jackson. Nevertheless, Jackson had agreed to act as a second for a friend in a duel with Benton's brother, Jesse. In 1813, Benton's grudge about this led him to accuse Jackson of insulting Jesse. Jackson and Benton argued in public and soon their disagreements exploded into outright warfare at a Nashville hotel.

The facts of the encounter were never clear, but the argument turned into a brawl between Jackson and his friends and Benton and Jesse. Some say Jackson shouted, "Defend yourself, you damned rascal" at Thomas Benton, but what happened next included gunshots, knives, fists, and finally Benton falling down a flight of stairs, bleeding from minor knife wounds. Jackson was struck by a bullet in the arm and nearly bled to death. Jesse Benton was wounded in the buttocks, but Benton claimed victory in the affair.

The encounter was the subject of much ridicule in Nashville, and after the war Benton realized his career in Tennessee had ended. He moved to St. Louis in 1815 and soon became a leading member of the St. Louis bar. But his temper had not improved, and in 1817 he clashed with Charles Lucas, a St. Louis man, over a court case. Benton challenged Lucas to a duel and at their first meeting, Lucas was seriously wounded. He recovered, but Benton continued to demand satisfaction. Eventually Lucas agreed to another encounter, and this time he lost his life to Benton, dying September 27, 1817, two days after his twenty-fifth birthday.

Benton ran for the Senate once Missouri gained statehood but faced the political ire of Charles Lucas's father, J.B.C. Lucas, a prominent judge in St. Louis, who attempted to stop Benton's political rise. During the election, Benton backers needed one more vote to elect him. This came from a dying man, who reportedly was carried into the political chamber on his bed to cast the deciding vote. Benton's support of Missouri statehood resulted in his election to the Senate, where he campaigned for a currency backed by silver and gold.

But perhaps Benton's most passionate cause was for the territorial expansion of the United States, what he saw as the country's "manifest destiny," its right to expand across the continent. Hating the land speculation of the time, he originated the policy of homestead laws, encouraging settlement of the frontier, and spoke out tirelessly for the settlement of western lands.

Benton immediately understood the value of the Santa Fe trade to Missouri economy: if New Mexico could provide bars and coins of silver, then it was a country to be courted. He later worked behind the scenes and on the Senate floor to obtain funding for a Santa Fe Trail survey, although he was blocked from developing a permanent military escort for traders. Benton knew the trader Augustus Storrs and the soldier/journalist/trader Alphonso Wetmore. Along with John Scott, a congressman from Missouri, Benton encouraged the men to write reports on the early trade and its effect on Missouri. Wetmore's response, based on interviews with men like Benjamin Cooper, is considered the first history of the Santa Fe Trail. Storrs participated in an expedition to Santa Fe and provided firsthand information about the region.

One of Benton's most famous quotations reflected his personality: "I never quarrel, sir; but I do fight, sir; and when I fight, sir, a funeral follows." Benton's belief in the trail's importance to Missouri won the fight in spirit, if not always in fact.

Another prominent influence on the Santa Fe trade was Dr. John Sappington. Maryland born and Tennessee raised, he had moved to the Boonslick in 1817. Although he never undertook a trip to Santa Fe himself, he was to have a positive impact on those who did. Sappington was an unusual physician for his time. The general medical belief was that patients should be made to purge and bleed (by cutting a vein) to rid them of disease. If the patient survived those treatments, he or she was then given stimulants to restore the body's balance. Sappington felt there were safer approaches to treatment. He spent much time observing and researching the uses of medicines and medical procedures. Malaria, called the ague at the time, was an endemic illness along the frontier. Soldiers and civilians frequently died from the effects of the debilitating disease, while others suffered alternate attacks of chills and fevers for years afterward, never knowing when they would be afflicted. Bennett Riley, the first military commander on the Santa Fe Trail, wrote to a friend of his experiences with malaria:

> I have had the fever from the first of October untill the 15th of January and am but just recovering from its effects . . . strange as it may seem, I performed a tour to franklin and back again through the prarie [sic] and wilderness a distance of about eight hundred miles . . . I was So Sick Some times that I hardly new any Person that was in company with me.

Some people believed malaria (an Italian word meaning "bad air") was caused by "miasmas" or damp fogs that arose from water or swamps. Although mosquitoes were a constant pest on the prairie, no one in the 1820s yet understood that malaria was spread by the mosquito's bite. Sappington knew from his reading and research that Jesuit missionaries in Peru had learned of a chemical called quinine from the native people. The chemical was extracted from tree bark called Peruvian or Jesuit bark. If given to a patient in precise doses at specific times during an attack of malaria, quinine could lessen or even stop the symptoms. The patient had to drink a vile-tasting extraction made by soaking Peruvian bark in whiskey or wine. "Bark and wine" was bitter but it did the job. It also led to frontier humor. Alphonso Wetmore wrote about a Boonslick woman with the ague. When told she needed the "bark and wine" for her illness, she couldn't understand why sounding like a dog would help but she was willing to give it a try. Wetmore penned a rhyming description of the ague for the *Missouri Intelligencer:*

> A painful yawn his muscles draw,
> projecting out under jaw,
> While chills run up and down his spine
> To indicate that bark and wine
> Must swell the list of human ills
> And follow up cathartic pills.

Early traders on the Missouri Trail carried the bark with them but the foul-tasting beverage often made the patient as sick as the malaria. In the 1830s, John Sappington invented "Sappington's Anti-Fever Pills," compounded of quinine, myrrh, and licorice. He explained his methods in *The Theory and Treatment of Fevers* in 1844: "The pills which author has prepared for sale . . . were simply composed of one grain of quinine each, three-fourths of a grain of liquorice, and one-fourth grain of myrrh, to which was added just so much of the oil of sassafrass as would give them an agreeable odor." Here was a cheap and simple way to prevent malaria. So popular did the pills become that a popular rhyme declared "Quinine, quinine is our cry, Give us quinine or we die."

Sappington was scorned by many doctors of the time for his innovations, but he succeeded with the public: millions of the pills were sold from Missouri to Texas, and few traders would attempt to travel the Santa

Fe Trail without stopping to buy enough to last the journey. William Becknell became a salesman for the pills later in life, and Sappington's son-in-law, Miles Meredith Marmaduke, a Santa Fe trader and later governor of Missouri, was well supplied with the pills on the Marmaduke-Storrs trip to Santa Fe.

While the doctor saved the lives of many others, he suffered the loss of three daughters from illness or childbirth. All three daughters had married the same man—Claiborne F. Jackson, who, like Marmaduke, became a governor of Missouri. A story of the time says that when Jackson came back to ask Sappington's permission to marry the last daughter, the doctor replied, "You can marry her, but don't come back for the old lady." Sappington's blunt humor was typical of the era, and he was respected and honored by the people of the Boonslick until his death in 1856. Although he never saw Santa Fe, he made it possible for many to do so in better health.

Augustus Storrs was born and raised in New Hampshire. A graduate of Dartmouth College, Storrs taught in New York but headed west to Missouri in 1814. He settled in Franklin, where he served as the postmaster and later as a government clerk. Not content to watch his neighbors head west, Storrs also became a trader. He traveled the trail with the Stephen Cooper-Marmaduke caravan and possibly again between 1823 and 1824. The 1824 Marmaduke-Storrs caravan was the largest to date, with 81 men (including slaves), 156 horses and mules, and 23 wagons and lighter carriages. The men also traveled with a piece of field artillery in case of attack by hostile Indians. (In some accounts, the artillery was old and rusted; in others, the gun was fired as a warning rather than with any hope of hitting an attacker.)

By the time of the Storrs caravan from Franklin, the Santa Fe trade's success was well known in Washington. Missouri governor Alexander McNair asked Congress to help develop the prairie trade and protect the traders on their journey. McNair and Senator Benton realized they must convince the rest of the country that the Santa Fe Trail was worth an investment by the American people. And who, asked Benton, would be the best spokesmen for the trail than Missourians? Benton traveled to the Boonslick as did John Scott, a representative from Missouri, where they met with men who knew or traveled the trail. Among them were Augustus Storrs and Alphonso Wetmore. Within a year, Wetmore wrote

FORT OSAGE - 1808 - JACKSON COUNTY

Fort Osage was named for the Native American people who lived and hunted along the Osage River and across Missouri. William Clark selected the site for the fort, noting that it would control access to the upper Missouri River. President Thomas Jefferson hoped the fort-trading post would keep peace on the frontier and be the beginning of a new era in trade relations between Native Americans and the United States. George Sibley, the factor at Fort Osage, was well informed about conditions along the trail to Santa Fe and offered helpful advice to William Becknell and later traders. This mural from the Missouri state capitol, painted by William Knox, shows the fort in 1808. (State Historical Society of Missouri, Columbia, Courtesy Hammond and Iwin, Jefferson City, Missouri)

the first history of the trail and Storrs answered a series of questions from Benton about conditions on the trail. On January 3, 1825, Benton addressed Congress and quoted from Storrs's document, calling Storrs "a gentleman of character and intelligence, every way capable of relating things as he saw them, and incapable of relating them otherwise."

Storrs offered careful and detailed answers about the Missouri and Santa Fe Trail. He described how, in order to cross streams, they had to "dig the banks down with spades and hoes and in some instances to cover the bottom with saplings and brush." Storrs explained that "deer are scarce, but buffalo, elk and antelopes are abundant. Buffalo meat is, generally, esteemed superior to beef; and that of the antelope, both in flavor and appearance, has a strong affinity to mutton." He commented on the landscape, sand hills, wildflowers, and the great, tall grasses of the prairie that were higher than a man on horseback.

Augustus Storrs's report helped Benton convince Congress to set aside funds for a survey of the trail. Perhaps this assistance, along with his skills, gained him the appointment as consul at Santa Fe. Storrs eventually took Mexican citizenship, set up a trading business, and moved to Texas, where he died in 1850 at age fifty-nine.

George Champlin Sibley, factor at Fort Osage, had been born into a Massachusetts family in 1782. His father, John, served in the American Revolution and later as an Indian agent in Natchitoches, Louisiana. His mother, Elizabeth Hopkins, was a minister's daughter and of an old New England family. John Sibley's connection with Thomas Jefferson resulted in George's appointment as assistant factor, or manager, of the Indian trading post, Fort Bellefontaine, outside of St. Louis. When the upright Sibley questioned the careless record-keeping methods at the post, he was fired for insubordination, but, determined to clear his name, he rode to Washington, defended himself before the Superintendent of Indian Affairs, and won a better position as the factor at Fort Osage when it was established in 1808.

Sibley's job was to trade with the Indians, avoid clashes with the military leaders posted to the fort, and deal with traders who resented government competition for furs and trade goods. Although a difficult mission, Sibley did it with determination and pride. He was a careful, fair, and honest man who treated the Indians with more understanding and respect than most factors and government representatives. The post was the farthest western fort at the time, on the edge of the frontier. Few people stopped there outside of soldiers, fur traders, and Indians, but this did not deter Sibley from bringing his fifteen-year-old bride, Mary Smith Easton, to the post in 1815. Mary was unfazed by frontier life: she brought with her furniture, books, and a piano with a fife and drum attachment that added a military zest to the performance. Her "concerts" entertained soldiers, frontiersmen, and Indians.

As early as 1821, Sibley welcomed Santa Fe traders to Fort Osage, but he had learned about the opportunities for Mexican trade much earlier.

Sibley's friend Dr. John Robinson had traveled with Zebulon Pike to Mexico in 1809, only to be arrested and thrown into a Spanish jail on charges of spying and entering the country illegally. Despite his situation, Robinson did not waste his time in Mexico but collected information and prepared maps about the region. Upon his release he served as a physician at Fort Osage and then was appointed Indian agent. Since both Sibley and Robinson understood the frontier, the doctor must have shared information about the Southwest with Sibley that served him well in his next government appointment.

In 1825, President John Quincy Adams named Sibley to a commission to survey the Santa Fe Trail. The survey had been guided through the Senate by Senator Benton, who believed that a marked and surveyed trail would increase trade and make it simpler to provide military escorts to protect the traders from Native American raids. Sibley knew that the relationship between emigrants and Native Americans had changed greatly since the frontier moved west of the Mississippi River. Where Indians had once been impressed by the threats of "no trade" from officials like Sibley, by the 1820s Osage, Kansas, Pawnee, and other tribes had obtained enough horses and guns that they could take goods rather than trade for them. In some cases, traders were merely stripped of their goods and horses; in other cases, they were beaten or killed.

Senators from the East and South did not care what happened in the West as long as the cotton and whaling trades were uninterrupted, but Benton insisted upon a survey with an eye towards securing the West for the future. He succeeded and Sibley became a member of the survey commission that included Benjamin Reeves, who resigned his position as lieutenant governor to accept the post. Adams appointed Pierre Menard as third commissioner, but he resigned and Reeves and Sibley appointed Joseph Brown as surveyor and Archibald Gamble, Sibley's brother-in-law, as secretary, leading to some complaints.

The survey began June 22, 1825, when Sibley left St. Louis for Fort Osage. Wagon breakdowns, hot weather, and prairie flies made travel difficult and slow. Sibley arrived in Franklin in time to join the Fourth of July celebration and offered a toast to warm the hearts of all present: "A few years since, I saw it [the Boonslick] a trackless wilderness; now it is the left arm of the state." In a few weeks, Sibley placed mile marker 1 of the Santa Fe Trail at Fort Osage. The survey, an amazing accomplishment, ended in 1826 despite political and other delays, including a lightning strike on Sibley's tent. He described the survey as "fraught with difficulties, privations and hazards innumerable."

Alphonso Wetmore was also from a New England family. He was born in Winchester, Connecticut, in 1793, the fifth of ten children. By 1803, the Wetmore family had moved to New York's Mohawk Valley. Little is known of Alphonso's boyhood, although his writings hint at a classical education. Wetmore joined the military in 1812 with his friend Robert Morris. Both young men courted the same woman, Mary Smith, and before they left for war, they gambled for a miniature portrait of Mary. Wetmore won. Within months, Morris had died in battle and Wetmore lost his right arm to cannon shrapnel. Despite the injury, he remained in the Army and was promoted to lieutenant. In 1813, he married Mary. He always believed that the miniature portrait he had won turned aside a bullet and saved his life.

By 1819, the Wetmores and their children had settled in Franklin and St. Louis, where he served as paymaster for the Army. In addition to his soldier's duties as troop paymaster, Wetmore was a journalist, writing essays and stories about life on the Missouri frontier and Santa Fe Trail. Missouri was not an easy post: Wetmore traveled constantly, moving from Nebraska to Washington, D.C., St. Louis to Philadelphia. He knew William Becknell, the Coles, and Coopers, but it took a disaster to set Wetmore on the path to Santa Fe. During a trip downriver on payroll duties, his raft broke up and sank during a thunderstorm. Although he made it to shore despite having only one arm, the troops' payroll was lost to the muddy Missouri. Wetmore had to repay the money to the U.S. government, a near impossibility on his salary. He traveled to New York, borrowed from his father to purchase trade goods, took a leave of absence in 1828, and set off for Santa Fe. He never allowed the loss of his arm to slow him down. Still a good shot with pistol and rifle, he was elected head of the caravan. In addition to his Santa Fe essays and history of the trail, Wetmore was author of the first gazetteer of Missouri and the first published playwright west of the Mississippi River.

Bennett Riley, born in Maryland in 1787, served as a rifleman in the War of 1812 and was posted to the frontier in 1819 along with the Sixth Regiment. He served with Alphonso Wetmore, was promoted to captain, and participated in peace talks with local Indian tribes. Wetmore wrote of traveling with Riley along the Missouri Trail; in one adventure, the men stayed at a log cabin with a family. The next morning, Wetmore and Riley decided to take a different route from the one they had planned and later discovered they had missed an ambush by the family's menfolk, who made a habit of waylaying visitors. Although a respected soldier and leader, Riley was a typical man of the times. Once, he was traveling by keelboat with another officer, Thomas Smith, and 200 enlisted men. They had been drinking and began to argue over whether a tree in the river was a snag or a sawyer. Smith and Riley agreed to a duel to settle the argument, and, ordering their men to steer to an island, the two disembarked, fired at each other, and climbed back in the keelboat, satisfied that their honor had been preserved.

Like Wetmore, Riley traveled the Santa Fe Trail, but not as a trader. He guided the first military escort along the trail in 1829 in an effort to protect the traders from Indian harassment. For this expedition Riley decided to use oxen instead of mules for the wagons. Everyone knew that mules had tougher hooves than oxen and could stand the heat on the plains better, but Riley showed oxen could pull greater loads. Traders realized that while oxen were slower than mules, the use of oxen would allow larger wagons and more trade goods per trip. Oxen could also provide beef if food became scarce, and the animals foraged for themselves while mules needed grain for feed, adding to the load. Soon, bullwhackers were competing with muleskinners along the trail and larger freight wagons helped the Santa Fe trade become a mainstay of the Missouri economy. Riley later took part in the Mexican War and served as the first military governor of California; he died in Buffalo, New York, in 1853.

One of the best known settlers in the Boonslick was John Hardeman, who had come to Franklin from Tennessee with his family and built a garden in the middle of the wilderness. His farm "Fruitage," several hundred acres along the Missouri, was near the present village of New Franklin. Hardeman was a farmer but wanted to do more than farm. Fruitage and another farm, "Penultima," near Jefferson City, were his pride and joy. In the 1820s, Hardeman cleared approximately nine square acres at Fruitage and laid out a formal garden with a central maze. To fill the garden, he imported fruits, trees, flowers, and shrubs from around the world. Letters to Hardeman show that he asked friends to collect seedlings and cuttings for his farm. George Sibley sent black and white grapes to Hardeman from

Mexico in 1826 while on the Santa Fe survey, warning him to protect the vines from frosts and cold winter weather. Captain Pentland of Council Bluffs wrote a lighthearted note saying he would keep an eye out on the prairies for curious plants. Both on the farm and in the garden, Hardeman hoped to demonstrate the agricultural possibilities of the frontier. As part of his campaign, he published a letter to Missouri senator Thomas Hart Benton, praising the fertile land and the region. He joked that Tennessee friends thought Missouri too cold for cotton. But, he boasted, cold was useful: the Devil once visited Missouri, caught a chill, and never returned.

Hardeman wrote that in addition to cotton, he raised Indian corn, grapes, cherries, apples, asparagus, radish, hemp, melons, squash, mustard, and Jerusalem artichoke. The fame of Hardeman's gardens drew many visitors, including Henry Shaw, who later founded the St. Louis Botanical Gardens. Hardeman believed that a band of trees around Fruitage would prevent the Missouri from flooding his land. Unfortunately, he was wrong, and much of his farm disappeared under the great floods of 1826 and 1827. The financial losses may have been one reason John Hardeman joined his friend Alphonso Wetmore as a trader to Santa Fe in 1828. He was a devoted father, and wrote to a friend about his trip, "I have strong hopes that it will enable me to spend the remainder of my days with my family." Once in Mexico, Hardeman traveled south, then boarded a ship for the return trip to New Orleans. There, he died of yellow fever in September 1829. According to a Boonslick legend, for many years a large rosebush bloomed along the banks of the Missouri River, the only survivor of John Hardeman's gardens.

The founder of the first newspaper west of St. Louis, Nathaniel Patten was born in Massachusetts, where he worked as a newspaper editor. He established a newspaper in Kentucky before heading west to Franklin, Missouri, in 1818. He was a small, frail man, who was nearly deaf by middle age. Patten began the Franklin newspaper in partnership with a Virginian, Benjamin Holliday. As with many newspapers of the time, its name was long and descriptive: the *Missouri Intelligencer and Boonslick Advertiser*. The first issue went on sale in April 1819 with the hope that "public measures and the public characters and acts of individuals in office will always be considered just subjects of investigation; but no private quarrels or the aspersion of private characters, will find admission into the columns of the *Intelligencer*." Patten hoped the newspaper would contribute to public policy and enlightened discussion as Missouri became a state. He printed local, national, and international news, although the mail took weeks to arrive from St. Louis and there were some issues where Patten apologized for the lack of stories, announcing once "we have no news." Although from a free state, Patten published many advertisements seeking the return of runaway slaves and announcing the sale or lease of men, women, and children.

From its beginning, the *Intelligencer* was praised by readers and publishers for the careful writing, but the newspaper struggled to cover its debts. Franklinites read the articles and advertised their wares and services but paid for their subscriptions in produce: Patten accepted pork, flour, and wood. Despite the obstacles, the paper eked out an existence. It was in the *Intelligencer* that William Becknell announced his plans for a hunting and trapping trip to the West. After the men returned safely and in triumph from Santa Fe, Patten continued to print many stories about the trade. He printed William Becknell's journals (after adding his own literary flourishes.) And it was the *Intelligencer* that printed an advertisement from an employer seeking a runaway apprentice named Christopher Carson. This was Kit Carson, who became one of the most famous explorers of the Far West. His employer offered a one-cent reward for Kit.

Patten's life was one of challenge and tragedy. Because the newspaper could not pay for itself, he worked as postmaster. When the post office was robbed, he was held responsible for repaying the missing $800. He supported his mother and sisters, who had moved to Missouri after his father died. When Franklin was flooded by the Missouri River, Patten moved the newspaper office to Fayette and then Columbia. He became the target of political attacks for his editorials and suffered personal attacks for his progressive politics. But even as other newspapers competed with and eventually overshadowed the *Intelligencer,* Patten continued to write about his adopted state, politics, and the Santa Fe trade. He died in 1837 at the age of forty-five, shortly after founding a newspaper in St. Charles, Missouri.

Under the Missouri Compromise, Missouri had entered the Union as a slave state, but some slaves were allowed to purchase their freedom and that of their families, which took years of work, saving, and hope. Perhaps the most famous free black to be associated with the Santa Fe Trail was Hiram Young of Independence. Born into slavery in Tennessee, Young was brought to Springfield, Missouri. in the early 1800s. By 1847 he was in Jackson County, having purchased his freedom from George Young for $1,500—nearly double what Young had paid for him. According to one account, Hiram earned the money by making and selling ox yokes. He had also purchased his wife Matilda's freedom, which he may have done first to ensure that their children were born free.

Young was a craftsman whose wagons and yokes were well known on the trail. He set up in business on Liberty Street in Independence where he continued to make yokes and eventually turned to making wagons. Young built a busy and successful business, with twenty-five forges and at least fifty employees, who reportedly built between 800 and 900 wagons a year. He hired free blacks, immigrants, and white workers for his factories. He also leased slaves from their owners or purchased slaves outright. He paid all the men the same wage, $5 per day, regardless of their color. This was done so that a slave could earn enough to buy his freedom and use the skills that Hiram Young taught him to create a new life as a free man.

The Hiram Young wagons were well made. Santa Fe trader William B. Napton wrote in 1857,

> The wagons were heavy, cumbrous affairs with long deep beds, covered with sheets of heavy cotton cloth, supported by bows. A man six feet high could stand erect in one of them, and they were designed to hold a load of seven or eight thousand pounds of merchandise each. Those in our train were made by Hiram Young . . . and they were considered as good as any.

Young's well-crafted wagons helped him obtain military contracts and were also purchased by many white Santa Fe traders. One of the most notorious was "Jim Crow" Chiles, a hot-headed, vicious man known for his temper and fists. His nickname was taken from a popular minstrel song. Minstrel shows featured white performers who painted their faces black with burnt cork and performed derisive versions of black music and dance. Chiles did not respect blacks, but he did purchase Hiram Young wagons.

Young's success was ended by the Civil War, but he was one of the few free blacks to succeed in Missouri before emancipation. Perhaps one measure of his association with the Santa Fe trade was that upon his death in 1882 he was buried in Woodlawn Cemetery in Independence, near the graves of white Santa Fe traders.

Of all the people who wrote about the Santa Fe Trail, Josiah Gregg is perhaps the best known. His book, *Commerce of the Prairies,* was published in 1844, but he had traveled the Missouri and Santa Fe trails beginning in 1831. The book was a history and a guide and business plan for those on the trail. It was Gregg who called Franklin the cradle of the Santa Fe trade, and *Commerce* is still an important source for historians. Gregg was born in 1806 in Tennessee, but moved near Fort Cooper in the Boonslick with his family. As a young boy, he experienced the loss of an uncle during an Indian attack and the kidnapping of a cousin, who managed to escape by grabbing a knife from her captor, slashing the ropes that tied her, and slipping off a galloping horse.

Later, the Greggs moved to a farm near Independence. Gregg was well educated and planned to be a lawyer and a teacher. But he suffered from "consumption," tuberculosis, and was told by the family doctor to go farther west or perish. Gregg thrived in the West. He traveled throughout Mexico, studied Spanish, and eventually became a trader. He mapped part of the trail, kept notes about the natural environment, and published *Commerce of the Prairies.* Gregg traveled across the prairies at least eight times. Later in life he received a medical degree and practiced as a doctor. He served as a translator for the military, a storekeeper, explorer, and newspaper correspondent. In 1850 Gregg was on an expedition in California when he collapsed and died of exhaustion. *Commerce of the Prairies* outlived its author but not his spirit of adventure that endures in the book.

Not all women who played a role in trail history visited Santa Fe; some had to set the stage for the great adventure. Hannah Cole of Boonville was the mother of an early Santa Fe trader and related to another. (Both men were killed in an ambush less than 100 miles from Santa Fe in 1823.) But Hannah made her own contributions to the Boonslick and the trail. In fact, without her help, Franklin and Boonville may have disappeared from the land.

Early in 1810, Hannah, her nine children, and her slaves Lucy and Isaac arrived at the site of what would become Franklin. Only a few weeks before, she had been widowed at age forty-nine when her husband was killed while searching for Indians who had stolen some horses. It is not known why, but Hannah and her family chose to settle on the south side of the river, across from Franklin and away from other families. The Coles were able to cross the Missouri and choose a cabin site near modern day Boonville, but a winter storm came up suddenly. They were stranded on the south side, while their wagon with food and equipment was on the north. After eleven days, the Coles canoed across, took apart the wagon, and transported everything back to their property. For the first few months, the family lived in a dwelling made of bark and saplings, but eventually Hannah and her family built a fort for protection during the War of 1812. At one time or another, the fort served as a post office, a home, the county seat, the courthouse, and a voting place. She and her sons ran a ferry service across the Missouri, and she bought and sold the land that became the town of Boonville. Hannah died at eighty-one in 1843 and was buried near Lucy, south of Boonville.

One of the most unusual accounts of a traveler on the Santa Fe Trail began in St. Louis. On September 16, 1847, a young Missouri soldier enlisted as a private in Company D of the Missouri Volunteers, part of the Santa Fe Trace Battalion commanded by Lt. Col. William Gilpin, a friend of Thomas Hart Benton. The new private spent a month training in weaponry, drills, and military discipline and learning about the grueling life of a soldier. In October, the unit began its journey down the Santa Fe Trail towards winter encampment in Colorado with plans for a spring march into Santa Fe. Although the private was known to his comrades as William Newcum, in truth "he" was Elizabeth Caroline Newcum, a twenty-two-year old Missouri adventurer.

Much of Elizabeth Newcum's life is a mystery. She lived in Missouri at the time of her enlistment, but whether she was born or raised in the state is unclear. She was unmarried when she enlisted. But somewhere and at some time she met and was wooed by a young man who hatched an unusual plan for his lady love. First Lieutenant Amandus V. Schnabel was a twenty-three-year old officer in Company D who enlisted on the same day as Elizabeth. Schnabel had emigrated from Germany with his family as a teenager, and his father, a physician, settled in St. Louis. From military and court records, it appears Schnabel convinced Elizabeth to enlist, pose as a man, and serve in Schnabel's unit so they could maintain their relationship. As an officer, Amandus was able to assign Elizabeth duties in his quarters, which helped her avoid being discovered. Disguised she may have been, but Elizabeth did not shirk her duties. She appears to have trained with her unit and traveled with them along the northern Santa Fe

Trail route to Colorado. She may have even participated in battles with the unit in the spring of 1848.

But by May 1848, Elizabeth was pregnant. One story claims that Amandus encouraged her to desert, but after hiding in a wagon heading east Elizabeth changed her mind and returned to her unit. By May 1848 Elizabeth was "discharged . . . discovered to be a disguised woman at Fort Leavenworth." Amandus was court-martialed for his role in the deception, partly on the grounds that he denied the military the services of a soldier! He returned to St. Louis and his family, and little was heard of him in later years.

Elizabeth, however, was made of sterner material. In 1853, a married Mrs. Elizabeth (Newcum) Smith filed a claim in Platte County, Missouri, for back pay as well as 160 acres of bounty land due to soldiers who served in the Mexican War. At least one soldier testified on her behalf, and identified her as Bill Newcum. It took a year, but in 1854 a special bill was passed by Congress that stated that Elizabeth was entitled to service pay, three months' extra pay, and the land "for her services as a Private." Elizabeth Newcum—mother, Missourian, and soldier—was only the second woman granted a pension for serving in the military. She was certainly the first female soldier to travel the Santa Fe Trail, and one of only a handful of trail women whose names are known to history.

CHAPTER 3

Life on the Trail

—⬬—

I crossed the Missouri and joined a large train,
Which bore us o'er mountains and valleys and plains;
And often at evening out hunting we'd go
To shoot the fleet antelope and wild buffalo.

From *Cowboy Songs and Other Frontier Ballads,* John A. Lomax (1911)

A SANTA FE TRADER STEPPED ONTO THE TRAIL and found an even more rough and tumble new world than the frontier. The trip from Franklin to Westport was roughly 150 miles, at least a week's travel in good weather. Once a trader was on the prairies, he was alone for months with only the men of his caravan for companionship. A common frontier saying was that all a man needed to survive was a good rifle, a good dog, and a good wife. A trip down the trail demanded much from everyone involved. Families were separated, wives left to wait and wonder about their men until a caravan or trapper returned. Alphonso Wetmore wrote a humorous sketch of an Arrow Rock wife married to a trapper. Her husband recalled, "She desired that I would write her, if any thing happened . . . She said it wouldn't bring me to life if the Indians scalped me, or I should starve, or freeze, or get drowned, or be struck with lightning, or chawed up by a grizzly bear; but it would be such a satisfaction to know I died easy." Wetmore's humor does not hide the fact that in the 1820s, travel from Missouri farther west was neither easy nor safe.

Once the caravans moved out, men and animals settled into the rhythm of travel. On a spring day, when a breeze caused the tall grasses

57

The buffalo provided food, clothing, blankets, rope, tipis, boats, and many more items to the Native and frontier hunters. At one time, millions of buffalo ranged across the prairies and plains, but hunters along the Santa Fe Trail helped to decimate the animals. Although the scientific name is "bison," most travelers referred to the game as buffalo, a word for wild ox. (Courtesy Missouri Department of Natural Resources, photo by Larry Larson)

and flowers to dip and sway and the clouds to scud along, the prairies must have resembled an inland sea to men bred along rivers, lakes, or ocean. Trees dotted the horizon here and there, islands of shade and landmarks in the middle of waving grasses. Pilot Grove, Missouri, got its name because prairie travelers took their bearings from a grove of trees there. Few Santa Fe Trail travelers noted their Missouri surroundings, but Duke Paul of Wuerttemberg, who traveled the Missouri frontier in 1823, 1830, and 1850, wrote of the Missouri landscape: "The road to Pierre de la Fleche (Arrow Rock) . . . a distance of about 12 English miles from Franklin, led through a sparsely inhabited region. The forest consisted of beautiful trees spaced apart and a dense composite undergrowth of herb-like plants." The duke was also entranced by a swamp filled with water

The Osage were noted by European visitors for their height, strength, and beauty, in addition to their trapping and hunting skills. This mural by E. Irving Couse is from *The State Capitol of Missouri,* Jefferson City, 1928. (State Historical Society of Missouri, Columbia)

lilies and alive with wood ducks and waterfowl. But the forests gave way quickly to open prairie, and Santa Fe traders had a saying that came from sailing: once men and horses reached the prairies, they were "out of sight of land." They were in the world of the trail.

Traders traveled together for companionship and safety. The farther a man traveled from Franklin, the more likely he was to meet with the tall and dignified Osage, or a group of Kaw or Fox and Sauk. Later, the Comanche, Pawnees, Apache, and Navajos appeared. Native tribes soon saw their land titles "extinguished" once they agreed to share the region with white settlers. Forced to move farther west, to poorer land, they were often reduced to begging for food and necessities. As the trail traffic increased, the competition for game animals also increased, although the wholesale extinction of species like the buffalo was only beginning. The clash of cultures brought tragic conflicts between Indians and settlers at the same time Missouri and Plains tribes faced increasing pressure from tribes moving in from the north and southeast. Seasonal hunting forays became less profitable and more dangerous. Santa Fe traders were soon moving thousands of oxen, mules, and horses up and down the trail. The foraging animals ate much of the grass along the paths, forcing Indians,

Mexicans, and whites to look farther afield for grazing areas. Springs and ponds were polluted with animal droppings. Groves of trees that had served as refuge from storms and hunger were chopped down for wagon axles or to serve as emergency feed for horses. Desperation led many natives to see the caravans as sources of supplies.

But the clashes went beyond resources. The War of 1812 was still alive with memories of battles and murders that had taken place. To many white traders, Indians were Indians, not distinct tribes with individual personalities. Traders could expect to meet Ioways, Arapahoes, Comanches, Pawnees, Blackfoot, Nez Perce, Osage, Navajo, Cheyennes, and Kiowa as well as others. Some were less warlike than others; some were known to torture captives; other tribes treated traders with respect and kindness, sharing food and lodging. (Alphonso Wetmore counted at least one Indian chief among his frontier friends.) Tales of kidnapped women and children who were mistreated or forcibly adopted into tribes added to the negative attitudes about Native Americans. Murders and attacks by both sides along the trail were often unprovoked and unexpected.

An early trail historian noted the traders "were in a great measure to blame for the treacherous conduct of the Indians. They would cheat and often kill in cold blood every Indian who came near the camp, even when he was friendly and intended good rather than harm." Neither side trusted the other. And no trading party ever felt secure. A traveler wrote of the trail as it left Missouri: "The road is a track where the grass does not [grow], winding like a snake, generally on the highest ground so that you can see a man for miles ahead of you like some dark object between you and horizon. All you have to do is to conceive a vast, dark elevated plain." Along that snake trail, caution and fear were constant companions.

When a trader set out in the 1820s, he took as few personal goods or "necessities" as possible. The more trade goods carried, the higher the profit. So except for a pot or pan and some medicines, the Missouri traders carried most of what they needed on their backs. Men of the time owned few pieces of clothing, some of it homemade, some store bought. Unless the trader was well to do and a bit of a dandy, most clothing was hard-wearing and practical year round, whatever the weather. Trousers were made of wool or jeans cotton, and fastened with buttons. "Overalls" were long trousers that buttoned over the shoe in order to keep out stones and brush; they were adapted from the military uniform of the day. The flannel or cotton shirt was full, long, and loose. It served as outer garment, sleeping garment, and underwear—the long shirt was tucked between the legs in place of drawers. Socks were hand knit and heavy to prevent calluses and blisters from heavy boots. Men sometimes wore deerskin moccasins, but that depended upon the terrain and on when shoes wore out along the trail.

For bad weather or the cold, there was a hooded coat made of heavy blanket wool (called a "capote"), and a hat. Depending upon a man's style, the hat could be a rounded bowler, a flat-brimmed "Quaker," or a woven straw. There were simple knitted hats of red yarn, like those of sailors or raftsmen. The most dramatic was the cap of animal skin, such as wolf or raccoon, with the tail intact. Daniel Boone is often depicted in a coonskin cap, but it is just as likely he wore a shaped felt or fur hat with a brim to shade his eyes. Alphonso Wetmore described the clothing of Boonslick men in his play, *The Pedlar*. The backwoods character Opossum wore a raccoon-skin cap, buckskin hunting shirt, and overalls. Old Prairie, who owned a cabin, wore "domestic dress" (trousers and a shirt) and a broad-brimmed hat. The Boatman wore a glazed leather hat, red flannel shirt, and linen overalls.

Samuel Wilson's description of trail clothing in 1849 shows that whatever a man owned he wore west:

> Their dress is as different and as whimsical as if they were dressed for a masquerade Ball. You will see every dress from undress blue frock coat of a military officer to the red fringed Hunting shirt of the backwoods. Some are dressed [in] uniforms . . . these and the almost universal slouched Sombero is a sure sign that the wares [wearers] are bound for the El Dorado.

The city of gold, El Dorado, was a legendary place somewhere in the New World. Perhaps Wilson is referring to real places, though: the wealth of either Santa Fe or the newly discovered California gold mines.

Shirts and leggings with fringe were practical: heavy buckskin and denim (named for the city of Nimes in France) stood up to the whipping of brush and high grasses. The fringe distracted flies and allowed rainwater to run off. When belted at the waist, the shirt became a handy place to carry necessities. Clothing, whether handmade or store bought, was valuable, and when it became tattered and torn, it was reused. A coat or jacket was cut down and reused as a vest. A scrap of cloth became a breech clout. The breech clout was borrowed from Indian clothing: the cloth went from the waist, down between the legs, and back up to the waist. It was held in place by a waist tie, and the man could wear high leather leggings to protect his legs. (As revealing as the breech clout was, mountain men and trappers did not worry about appearing in public.)

Clothing styles did not change rapidly on the frontier. Although the Santa Fe Trail opened nearly twenty years after the Lewis and Clark expedition and almost a dozen years after the War of 1812 convulsed the region, clothing still reflected an earlier time. The linsey hunting frock worn by the Coopers or Coles in 1811 was still useful on the trail. Linsey was linen fabric; linsey woolsey was a combination of linen and wool. Although "frock" now means a dress, in the past it meant a loose, long jacket belted at the waist. The hunting frock generally had a deep cape-like collar with fringed edges that shed water and added a layer of protection against weather. Frontiersmen dressed for survival in all weather, from a blizzard to the miserable humidity of a Missouri summer. Besides weather, the men had to defend against the bites and stings of green-headed flies, mosquitoes, ticks, and chiggers. The clothing had to be well made and maintained for it to do any good. Emigrants unskilled at preparing deerskin for use in moccasins, frocks, shirts, or leggings might find themselves with stiff clothing that clapped together like boards once the temperature dropped.

No man cared to go barefoot on the trail. Aside from stones, there were plenty of snakes and many of them poisonous. But perhaps the piece of clothing that caused the most trouble was shoes. In the 1820s, shoes were of heavy leather with thick soles. The soles were attached to the upper part of the shoe by nails or glue, which made for uncomfortable walking, especially walking 900 miles of trail. Once shoes and boots got wet, the men suffered from painful calluses, corns, and blisters. Moccasins were more comfortable and lighter to wear, and could be lined with fur, or thick plant leaves such as lamb's ear. But moccasins had to be made properly or the wearer found himself tortured by shrinking leather. Alphonso Wetmore wrote of one New Englander on the trail:

> Jonas was prone to new inventions, and he never would be content
> to make his moccasins like any other white man, with a good piece of

tanned deer-skin, and whang leather to sew them with. But in order to make a good fit, and ensure durability, he insisted that he would draw a piece of green hide over his feet. He went out to his traps in a pair of this sort; but after one trial he had no disposition to put his feet in a vice again.

At the men's sides hung their knives, bullet pouches, and powder horns. All had rifles. The Kentucky rifle was still popular in 1821: five feet or more in length, with a simple sight and a flintlock for firing, the weapon was heavy, but in the hands of a skilled hunter, it was a dependable companion. On the frontier, accuracy in shooting was absolutely necessary for protection and survival. Both Daniel Boone and wife Rebecca could pick off a deer with one rifle ball or "bark a squirrel off a tree." (To bark a squirrel was to shoot just below the animal at the tree bark. When the bark exploded, it either killed the squirrel or knocked it to the ground. According to some accounts, this preserved the pelt.) The older rifles had less kick and so could be fired by holding the weapon at the forearm and not at the shoulder. In skilled hands, this meant that the shooter revealed less of his body when firing from behind a tree or a wagon, a safer method when an enemy was firing back. The men—and women—of the trail were often equally skilled with firearms and woodlore.

Some rifles used on the Santa Fe Trail still used flints to create a spark that exploded the gunpowder and sent the ball and patch (bullet) out of the barrel. French powder was the most dependable, but locally made powder was available in the Boonslick from Joseph Jolly of Boonville. (Jolly's son was typical of the Santa Fe times: he worked as a wheelwright, gunsmith, cooper, blacksmith, miller, distiller, farmer, preacher, and doctor.) Men trusted their rifles to get them through dangerous times. Some even named their rifles: one man called his Sweet Lips because she sounded so pretty, while another called his rifle Old Bet, after a sweetheart named Betsy. Hunting and rifle phrases entered everyday language as well. A warning of "Keep your powder dry" meant to be careful. "Every shot a pigeon!" told someone to be cautious and not to waste his time (and bullets) and finally, "Pick your flint and try again!" meant to try new ideas in order to solve a problem. For the traders, "a flash in the pan" didn't mean something that was popular for a short time. The term meant

Richard Gentry was a politician, soldier, and Santa Fe trader. Born in Madison County, Kentucky, in 1788, he served in the Kentucky State Militia during the War of 1812. In 1816, he emigrated to Missouri with his wife and four young childen. He lived in Franklin for several years, and later moved to Columbia, where he owned a tavern, ran for public office, and served in the Missouri Militia. Gentry traveled to Santa Fe on at least two occasions and was among the first traders to bring mules back to Missouri, where they formed the basis for the famous Missouri mule stock. Serving in the Missouri Volunteers, he died from wounds suffered in a battle with the Seminoles in Florida in 1837. (State Historical Society of Missouri, Columbia)

Like many pioneer women, Ann Hawkins Gentry was alone with her children for long periods of time while her husband served in the militia or traveled to Santa Fe. After his death, left with thirteen children, she became postmistress in Columbia though the efforts of Senator Thomas Hart Benton, the second woman in the United States to hold that position. She became known for her efficiency, and each succeeding president, whatever his party affiliation, reappointed her to the position until she retired in 1868. She also managed the family tavern and took care of several grandchildren. She died in 1870 and is buried in the Columbia Cemetery. (State Historical Society of Missouri, Columbia)

that the flint "flashed," but the gunpowder had not ignited. During a fight, a flash in the pan could mean death.

But as necessary as guns were, they could cause as many problems as they solved. One Missouri trader, Andrew Broadus, suffered a near-fatal accident. Traveling with an 1826 caravan, he ignored commonsense safety rules and pulled his rifle out of the wagon by the muzzle. The gun went off, shattering his arm. Broadus refused to have his arm amputated, but infection set in and the situation became a choice between amputation or death. There was no doctor available, so Richard Gentry from Columbia used a carpenter's saw and a hunting knife to amputate the arm. The wound was sealed with a heated wheel bolt. Amazingly, Broadus recovered and continued to New Mexico. Ironically, Broadus had sued Gentry, a family friend, several years earlier.

During his trip to New Mexico, Alphonso Wetmore was selected the caravan's leader, or *caravanbachi*. Here, in fictional form, he describes facing down a tough trader on the Missouri Trail:

> "Disengage your team from your wagon instantly," said the captain, "and if you move a yard further ahead, I will give you a buck load." The fearless mutineer took the reins, evidently with the purpose of going ahead. Captain Rainmore raised his double barrel, drew back the cock of each lock, and looked steadily at his victim.

Wetmore also carried a pistol called a yager (from *Jaeger*, German for "hunter"). He noted that the need for weapons went beyond hunting and fighting: "The arms he carried were the substitutes for law and regulations," and he seems to have been a dead shot.

How much the men depended on their weapons is shown by Boonslick trader Stephen Cooper. On an 1822 trip to New Mexico, Cooper described a meeting with the governor of Mexico: "I told him I would not give up my arms any way. I had a rifle, a big knife suspended from my neck hanging down in front of me, and a large horse-pistol by my side." These precautions worked, and Cooper survived the trip.

There were other dangers and distractions on the Missouri Trail. The towns of Franklin and Boonville may have had hotels and warehouses, but it had been only a few years before 1821 that a panther measuring 11 feet from nose to tail tip had been killed in Boonville. Wolves and coyotes attacked horses and livestock that roamed free at night. Bears were seen along the trail, although they were black bears and not the great "white bear" or grizzly, so called because the bear's fur appeared to be tipped with white or "grizzled." Still, stories about bear attacks were told around campfires and printed by Nathaniel Patten in the *Missouri Intelligencer.* The most famous tale was about the trapper Hugh Glass, who was mauled by a grizzly bear while trapping on the Grand River in South Dakota in 1823. Left for dead by his associates, Glass regained consciousness, set his own broken leg, and began to crawl and walk 200 miles to the nearest settlement. He made it despite the injuries, and lived to find the men who abandoned him. Among them was M. M. Marmaduke, an early Santa Fe trader and future governor of Missouri, and Jim Bridger, who gained fame as a stalwart mountain man. Glass proved to be a better man than either of his associates: he took no revenge.

Not all encounters with wildlife were deadly. In "Sketch of Mountain Life," Wetmore wrote about a friend's wife who found her son playing with a young bear near their Arrow Rock cabin. Settlers believed that a bear would grab a person and choke the breath out of him, so the woman grabbed her rifle as the bear cub reached for her son. Just then, the mama bear appeared and charged the human mother, but a well-placed shot sent both bears running back to the forest and the boy to the cabin.

Wildlife did not have to be large in order to be dangerous or just plain annoying. Clouds of mosquitoes swarmed at dusk and dawn, keeping the men from sleep and transmitting malaria with a bite. The morning brought the green-headed prairie flies, a biting fly that swarmed around horses and traders, drawing blood with bites and causing both animals and men great discomfort. In extreme cases, the blood loss weakened the animals or drove them to break away from the pack train in a mad dash. Horses with docked, or trimmed, tails were provided with a false tail made of linen strings, but the flies often prevailed. George Sibley traveled from St. Louis to Fort Osage in 1825 on the Santa Fe Trail survey. He noted the flies:

Wednesday 29th June
The flies are very bad in all the Prairies above Mrs. Bailey's.

Thursday 30th June
The flies are so bad in the Grand Prairie that is impossible to travel

through it in the day without very great injury to the Horses. Even at
Harrison's we were obliged to keep the Horses Shut up in Stables. At
Sunset we left Harrison's, waggons & all. I got to Regan's at about 12 &
went to bed.

Sibley found it easier to travel by night and avoid the flies, although
night travel required either moonlight or torches and lanterns to light the
way. No matter how well marked a road, to move wagons and stock along
in the dark meant slow and careful travel or a wait for a full moon. All
because of flies.

In the first year of the Santa Fe Trail, Missourians took pack trains and
wagons to the west. By 1822, caravans were introduced as well. The word
"caravan" is Persian, and referred to a group of people traveling together
on a religious pilgrimage. The Santa Fe traders used it to mean a group
of trains or wagons that traveled together for safety on the plains. Each
caravan began with a rendezvous, where men gathered to organize their
goods, horses, mules, and wagons. Missouri traders came from all backgrounds. Some men, like Alphonso Wetmore and Miles Marmaduke,
were well educated. Others, like Becknell, could barely write their names.
There were English, Irish, and French. Later caravans included Mexicans,
Spanish, and Germans. Whatever their language and cultural differences,
the men all wanted to be part of a successful commercial trip to Santa Fe
and back.

In the early days, meetings were held in Franklin or Boonville. Later, as
the trailhead moved father west, a meeting place called Camp Rendezvous
was organized towards Independence. A camp allowed traders who lived
a distance away to plan their arrival, and caravans met at Independence,
Westport, and the Blue country, south of Kansas City near the Blue Rivers.
Rendezvous could take days or weeks as the men organized and waited
for supplies and good weather. Travel across Missouri was never easy,
even in later years. One man on his way by stagecoach to a rendezvous in
1853 telegraphed from Jefferson City to a friend complaining about Mr.
Fink's stagecoach service and saying he would meet the caravan as soon
as he could:

> Fink's stages are so rickety,
> His horses are so slow,
> His drivers are such drunken sots,

They scarce can make them go.
Then hold your horses, Billy,
Just hold them for a day;
I've crossed the River Jordan,
And am bound for Santa Fe.

As the Missouri Trail matured and moved west, it lost none of its allure and adventure. In 1846, Edwin Bryant set out for Santa Fe from Independence. His description of a send-off for traders reveals that even years after the Santa Fe trade had begun, it still had a great sense of adventure about it.

> The Masonic lodges of Independence commemorated the departure of their brother Masons connected with the Santa Fe and emigrating parties by a public procession and an address . . . A large audience was collected [and] the address was delivered . . . After the addresses an original hymn, written for the occasion was sung with much feeling by the whole audience to the tune of "Old Rosin the Bow."

At the rendezvous, a *caravanbachi,* or leader, was voted in by the traders. It was the leader's duty to get the caravan safely to Santa Fe. The *caravanbachi* chose the route, organized the group, started and stopped the caravan each day, kept order among the men, and commanded the group during Indian attacks or emergencies like stampedes or violent storms. But the traders and drivers were an independent group, and not always with the *caravanbachi.* The 1838 *Missouri Saturday News* contained a story by Alphonso Wetmore about one character, Mike Terrapin, who was unhappy with Wetmore as *caravanbachi* and warned the traders after the election of the leader. "Now boys . . . you think you're mighty smart in this ere election; but the way that regular officer will make you squar up will be awful. No sorta chance of sloping off to hunt buffalo."

Wetmore noted that men would obey laws only if they wanted to—or if they were threatened with a pistol. The safety of the caravan was the most important responsibility of all, and punishment for mutiny was severe. In rare cases, a man who put the caravan at risk was punished by being left alone on the side of the trail to make his way home alone as best he might.

A caravan's organization depended upon the mode of animal transportation. The early caravans used pack animals that walked single or double file across the prairies, following buffalo or deer traces through the grass. Wagon trains took up far more space and moved in two or even four lines. Once beyond Missouri and on the Plains, the danger from Indian harassment or stampedes increased. By driving in parallel lines, wagon trains could quickly pull into a square or circle for defense. If there was time, wheels were chained together, animals were moved inside the enclosure, and the wagons used as a fort. Beyond the Missouri River and onto the plains, Indian tribes such as the Pawnee or Comanches were famous for stealing horses and mules. While some Indian warriors galloped around the wagons and fired rifles and arrows into the air, others attempted to drive off the animals. Wetmore's caravan drove off such an attack by forming a circle, driving the animals into the camp and firing rifles and "the brass four pounder," a small cannon.

After these raids, traders were sometimes left with only a few horses or a single yoke of oxen. In some cases, traders were forced to return to Missouri on foot, more than a hundred miles. The U.S. government understood that Indian raids could destroy the lucrative Santa Fe trade, but little was done to help the traders until Senator Thomas Hart Benton prodded Congress to provide security for the trading parties. As an outcome of Benton's urging, Major Bennett Riley, a friend of Wetmore's and a frequent visitor to Franklin, was sent on a few occasions with troops to escort the traders along part of the trail. Riley also negotiated at various times with the tribes (and threatened them) to retrieve stolen horses and trade goods. A few traders ended up buying back their own horses from the tribes, but many men lost all their investments and got no return— except empty pockets and a long walk across the plains.

Some men had no choice but to walk, especially if they lost their horses or became stranded in bad weather. This is what happened to Missourians James Baird and Samuel Chambers in 1822 near present-day Dodge City, Kansas. A combination of an early winter and strayed animals left the men with no choice but to camp until spring and then walk a few hundred miles for new mounts. Since they had valuable furs and goods with them, the men dug holes and buried the items, which they retrieved on their way back to Missouri weeks later. A cache was not only to hold the goods, but to hide them from dishonest travelers. Josiah Gregg described how to dig a cache that would conceal things safely. First, find a slight rise or higher land, so rain will run off and not seep into the cache. Then dig a hole in the "shape of a jug" and line it with sticks and grass. Cover the items with more grass for protection, then replace the turf on it. If that is not possible, drive the animals over it to hide your work. Throw away any extra soil and grasses.

Traders who first traveled the Missouri and Santa Fe Trails knew only a little about the trail conditions. William Becknell and his caravan chose pack horses for the first journey, since this was the method of travel most familiar to them. It is possible that the men rode horses while leading packhorses, although later traders would walk most of the way, using the animals for work and not comfort. Horses were expensive, could not carry much in the way of goods, and did not have the stamina of animals like mules or oxen. Still, horses were used to difficult frontier life and work. John Peck wrote in 1819 that while on a missionary tour through Missouri he "found his horse was sick and lame. It was the same horse that had brought my family from the State of Connecticut to Shawneetown, Ohio, and which performed hard and valuable service through the summer and the autumn." Peck traveled at least 100 miles more "through timber and brushwood" to finish his preaching tour, making the "sick and lame" horse pick its way around the trees or jump over them. On a typical journey, horses might swim the rivers or cross "hurricanes," areas blown down by tornadoes or high winds, where trees and brush caused a rider to slow down to a walk. Given the harsh riding conditions and lack of decent food or stable, it is no wonder that others, including George Sibley and Josiah Gregg, noticed the ill and "jaded" or worn-out horses.

Forage in the form of grass and trees was found along the trail, but it took only a few years for the trade to destroy the trail's environment. As caravans grew to require hundreds of horses, mules, and oxen, and as thousands of Mexican mules were driven back north to Missouri, the region became overgrazed. Great stands of trees were cut down for firewood or wagon axles. Some Indian tribes were horse traders, with herds containing several thousand horses. All of this put enormous pressure on the land, with the result that good forage grasses could only be found farther and farther off the trail. When found, prairie grasses provided rich grazing. If an early winter or late spring storm struck the caravan, the animals pawed through the snow and ice. But long heavy snows could be disastrous and when no grass was available, branches were stripped from cottonwood and birch trees for the animals.

Christopher "Kit" Carson ran off in 1826 to join a caravan west. Since he had been apprenticed to David Workman, a saddle maker, after his father died, Kit could have been forced to return home and finish his time. Instead, Workman offered a (very) small reward for Kit, thus giving him a chance to get away. (State Historical Society of Missouri, Columbia)

In the later years of the trail, as towns such as Arrow Rock, Lexington, and Independence prospered, caravans in Missouri stopped at inns and taverns where the animals could be fed and watered and penned up for the night. Horse stealing was punishable by death, but that didn't stop the theft of hogs, cows, and good horses. If a horse or mule broke down—became injured or ill and unable to travel—it was let loose to fend for itself or exchanged for a more trailworthy companion. At least one trader wrote that horses left alongside the trail sometimes grew healthy and fat from the rest and the grass and were captured and used on the return trip.

Horses required bridles, saddles, and reins, and leather workers set up shop in Franklin, Boonville, and other Missouri Trail towns. One of the best-known saddlemakers on the Missouri Trail was David Workman of Franklin. Workman was born in England, and he emigrated to America in 1817 and settled on the Missouri River. He had ample business on the frontier and soon returned to England where he convinced his brother William to join him. By 1823, David also had an apprentice, Christopher "Kit" Carson, who ran off in 1826 to join his brothers on the trail. Although David Workman lost his assistant, he seemed to bear no grudge. Under the law, Workman was required to advertise for Kit's return, and he did so—weeks later:

> Notice is hereby given to all persons,
> That Christopher Carson, a boy about 16 years old, small of his age, but thick-set; light hair, ran away from the subscriber, living in Franklin, Howard County, Missouri, to whom he had been bound to learn the saddler's trade, on or about the first of September last. He is supposed to have made his way to the upper part of the state. All persons are notified not to harbor, support, or assist said boy under the penalty of the law. One cent reward will be given to any person who will bring back the said boy.

The advertisement is wrong on nearly all counts: Kit headed west, not north, he left in August, not September, and later descriptions call him slight, not thick-set. Certainly no one had the time to retrieve a runaway for the price of a penny. Good-hearted David Workman had given Kit a clear start on a new life. Workman seemed to have little luck when it came to keeping apprentices or partners: in 1825, his brother William had joined a Santa Fe caravan, leaving David behind. (Alphonso Wetmore wrote of an Englishman in his caravan who killed rattlesnakes, perhaps William Workman.) Within a few years, William became a naturalized Mexican citizen. He remained in New Mexico as a trader and distiller. David Workman traveled the trail himself with Ezekiel Williams and Augustus Storr in 1827, and remained a trader for nearly twenty years.

From his home in Franklin, Alphonso Wetmore wrote about the mule trains as the Missouri Trail developed. His article "The Book of the Muleteers" appeared in 1825 in the *Missouri Intelligencer* and poked fun at traders, comparing them to Joseph and his brothers of the Old Testament, who traveled into Egypt for grain. But even in fun, Wetmore made it clear that the traders were seeking valuable goods. "We come from afar . . . laden with merchandise and we seek gold and silver, the ox and the ass and all that is within thy gates." As the men returned to the

In his later years, Alphonso Wetmore owned a newspaper, practiced law, and ran for public office. His spirit of adventure never waned and in 1849 he visited California. When he returned to St. Louis, the great cholera epidemic was raging. It claimed nearly a quarter of the city's population, among them Wetmore. (Courtesy the Missouri History Museum, St. Louis)

Boonslick, they "gazed on the mighty sheet of angry waters and . . . cried out with one voice 'Missouri!' . . . And they were glad . . . for every one had many shekels of silver and horses and mules and ass colts."

Other animals sometimes traveled the trail with the traders. At least one Missouri caravan took hogs to provide food until the men reached Kansas and buffalo country. The treatment of animals varied with the caravan, although few animals had an easy life on the trail. Dogs provided protection and companionship, walking the thousand miles and more. That they suffered along with their masters is clear. On their trading trips, Alphonso Wetmore and Miles Marmaduke noted that some dogs died from thirst or dropped in their tracks from the intense heat.

Water was always a problem. The wagons carried water barrels, but never, it seemed, enough to get the men and animals past dry areas. Creeks and rivers afforded drinking water, but springs were the most desired by man and animal. One of the most famous sources was the Wagon Spring, or Santa Fe Spring, in Arrow Rock. Clear and strong, it still bubbles up and out into a stream singing its way over gravel. After a long day's ride, man and animal appreciated a good drink of clear water. At least one trader commented that he had to drink bad water so full of insects and plant life he "had to strain it through [his] teeth." The most dangerous "water scrape" or area without water, was the *jornada*. This region near the Oklahoma panhandle was one of the early wagon routes. Few springs or water sources were found along a sixty-mile length—which meant that a caravan might have to travel four or five days without enough drinking water. No matter how much water was carried, barrels soon ran dry, and animals stampeded to dry river beds hoping to scrape up a drop or two. Many traders suffered on this dry route. M. M. Marmaduke recalled that it was the only time along the trail that he was concerned about survival.

Alphonso Wetmore told a darker story. His caravan drank up its water only a few hours into the desert region: "It was difficult to enforce the orders which had been given to insure frugality in the use of water, and its scarcity induced many to consume it when not urged to drink by thirst, fearing they should not obtain a fair proportion." This had dire consequences. Within two days, the dogs had died, there was a near mutiny, and Wetmore was reduced to having his men sleep under the open sky so that they might catch any dew which fell. Some chewed bullets to stimulate saliva and keep their tongues from swelling. One man tried to kill himself but was too weak to pull a trigger. Wetmore doled out a few drops of vinegar, carried to prevent scurvy, not thirst, to each man as they trudged on. Finally, they came to a dry riverbed, and the few men who still had strength dug down until muddy water bubbled up. Other caravans survived by shooting buffalo and drinking the liquid found in the animals' stomachs. The dry route was a faster way to Santa Fe, but Missourians suffered much along that part of the trail.

In spite of the dry conditions, most traders could survive from the land. Becknell, an experienced Army ranger, instructed his men to bring "a horse, a good rifle . . . ammunition . . . and sufficient cloathing." A pot or pan for cooking, a knife for eating, and perhaps a blanket to sleep under was all anyone should need. Illness was dosed with a few simple medicines. Boneset, a wildflower, was gathered and brewed into a tea for the ague. Becknell used rhubarb, camphor, and whiskey to settle upset stomachs. The trappers and hunters called the liquid squeezed from a buffalo's gallbladder "mountain cider." A drink of these "bitters" was said to cure bad stomachs—if the drinker could keep the medicine down. Frontier survival skills were so necessary that the Reverend Peck was surprised at travelers along Missouri trails who had no common sense when it came to trail travel. Peck's comments about a man who nearly died during a snowstorm also offer a glimpse of how traders managed on the trail:

> We listened to the distressing tale with amazement! This man was . . . accustomed all his life to frontiers and yet had never learned one of the. . . . lessons of a backwoodsman . . . how all . . . who had to travel over uninhabited deserts made their camping place and kept themselves comfortable. The first thing is to select the right place, in some hollow or ravine protected from the wind, and if possible behind some old forest giant [tree] which the storms of winter have prostrated. And then . . . don't build your fire against the tree, for that is the place for your head and shoulders to lie, and around which the smoke and heated air may curl. Then . . . gather a quantity of grass, leaves and small brush, and after you have cleared away the snow . . . you may sleep comfortably. . . . wrap around you your blankets with your saddles for pillows . . . If it rains, a very little labor [placing pieces of] bark or even brush with the tops sloping downward will be no mean shelter. *Keep your feet straight to the fire* but not near enough to burn your moccasins or boots, and your legs and whole body will be warm.

Peck went on to repeat a guide for good life: "Keep your feet warm, your back straight, your head cool, and bid defiance to the doctors."

On the first part of the trail, traders could build a shelter from tree limbs and branches, but once on the open prairie, even that frail cover was gone. Not until larger wagons became standard trail equipment could a man sleep under or in one, safe from the elements. For Becknell, the Coopers, the Coles, and other early traders, staying dry was not always possible. Trail journals mention blizzards, floods, hail, rain, lightning, thunder, and windstorms. Men told of waking up surrounded by water or having their candles blown out in the wind, forcing them to sit out the storm in darkness. Hailstones big as rocks bloodied men and animals. Prairie fires sparked by lightning darkened the skies with billows of smoke, causing stampedes. Tornadoes were rarely mentioned, although one distracted a later caravan by picking up a wagon and spinning it in the air. (In the nineteenth century, a spinning cloud was called a cyclone or devil wind.) Possibly the most spectacular sky event on the trail occurred in 1833 when the Leonid meteorite shower filled the night with falling stars. Thousands of "stars" fell each hour. Some traders considered the event a bad omen, and many Missourians believed the end of the world was at hand.

Few records mention personal hygiene on the Missouri Trail and farther west. A dip in a stream was cooling on an August evening, but few men removed much clothing on a cold night. Hair was roughly cut, and many of the former soldiers knew how to shave in the field using a sharp knife for a razor and a pan of water as a mirror. When men suffered from stomach complaints and illness, they had no outhouses or privies, and were forced to move off into the brush or behind a wagon for privacy. (Later, when women were on the trail, some suggest men went to the left of the wagons and women to the right when necessary.) A man too weak from illness to ride his horse was a problem. The caravan could wait a day or two for him to recover some strength, but other times he was carried along in a wagon with little comfort or company during his illness.

But one other problem was dreaded on the trails: homesickness. The trader James Josiah Webb recalled a trip across the plains from Santa Fe to Missouri in 1845. The group—including two Mexicans—had a wagon, twenty mules, and two horses. They left in November and faced many hardships from snow to the icebound Arkansas River. The camp dog attacked Webb, the mules ran off, and one of the men stepped into prickly pear cactus and had to hop along on the search for the animals. During one night at camp, the cook began singing "Home Sweet Home," and the realization of their danger was too much for Webb. "I called him to order and offered a resolution that any member of the company who, during the balance of the trip, should sing any song of home or speak of the good things of home or of the comforts of home should be fined a gallon of whiskey payable on our arrival at Westport." Webb understood that men needed to remain focused on the matters at hand. Tender-heartedness, wrote Webb, had no place on the prairie.

Locating food on the Missouri Trail took a steady hand and a good eye. It also took common sense. The men carried some ingredients for making meals on the trail. According to both Josiah Gregg and James Webb, each man should bring fifty pounds of flour and bacon, ten pounds of coffee, twenty pounds of sugar, and some salt. Crackers, dried beans, or other goods could be carried, depending upon the number of pack animals available or the space in a wagon. A pot or pan in which to cook and a coffeepot made up the mess kit, although experienced mountain men and trappers could make do with less. Meals were eaten at daybreak or earlier, then at the "nooning," or midday break. Caravans stopped and set up camp before dark, and travelers enjoyed supper before turning in for the night.

Cooking was simple in good weather, but rain and damp resulted in poor campfires and cold dinners. A fire built with dried wood burned hot; green wood produced a slower, steadier fire; damp wood produced smoke and hunger. Buffalo chips burned quick, hot, and bright. Meat was roasted and broiled or barbecued over the fire, simple unleavened bread cooked in a pan or on a flat rock, and soup and coffee boiled. Indian tribes called the traders' coffee "muddy water." Liquor was drunk on and off the trail and believed to be healthier than water. Duke Paul of Wuerttemberg wrote during his Missouri Trail trip in 1823, "In this great heat, drinking water unmixed with some kind of spirituous drink is very harmful and may produce fever." It was not the heat that caused the problems but impure water, although the connection between the two was not yet understood. The effects of "spirituous drink" could cause unexpected problems. The duke complained that his crew had not been in Franklin an hour before the men were drunk and a fight began between the boatmen and the town ruffians.

Vegetables and fruits helped prevent diseases such as scurvy or "bad blood," thought to be from poor digestion and heavy diets. Wild greens, like watercress, went into the soup pot. Men spent time hunting for bee trees and honey. In 1826, Major Bennett Riley reported that his troops enjoyed "pork, beans, salt, vinegar, soap, candles and about twenty-eight days' of flour and bread" along with buffalo meat. During the trip, the officers met with a Mexican dignitary, Antonio Viscarra, and enjoyed dinners including salt pork, chocolate, fried ham, cake, and whiskey. Viscarra had also brought along china and silverware for dining. One of the most popular trail meals was a roasted marrowbone. According to a Missouri settler, the largest bones of a deer or buffalo were cooked over the fire, then cracked, and the men "filled a tin cup with marrow, salted it and ate it very heartily." Another delicacy was beaver tail. The men cooked it by slicing thin slabs of the meat and broiling it.

Although buffalo had disappeared from Missouri by 1821, the animal provided the bulk of meat for traders once they crossed the river into Kansas. One buffalo might feed a small caravan, but often an animal was killed only for its hump, considered the best cut of meat. If there was time, the men might prepare meat to carry along, thinly trimmed, hung along the sides of a wagon, and dried in the hot air. One Missouri hunter recalled drying meat: "We made a scaffold and laying the meat on small sticks built a fire under it and dried it. We also stretched the hides and dried them." Still, the waste was enormous. Often nine or more buffalo were killed to feed eighty men, more than double the number of animals necessary. The untreated, or green, hides were generally left to rot, unless needed for a saddle blanket or a "bull boat." This was an easily constructed boat used to cross lakes or shallow rivers. Wetmore described the boats, which could be made from any large hide, including elk:

> We crossed the Kanzas [Kansas River] low down, and ferried over our beaver in a *beaucoup*. This is a skin-boat, to which the French traders applied the word in their language signifying "much, abundance." In it, they were accustomed to convey at once, across a stream, all the baggage of a small traveling party. The boat is formed by running a small cord around the outer edge of the skin; and when this is drawn, the baggage distends the skin so as to make it buoyant.

The skin was laid on the ground, then tied and laced around a framework of pliant branches. When the boat was picked up, it was shaped like a bowl. The boats could be loaded ashore or afloat, and they were light enough for one person to carry. Indians used bull boats, and it is possible that trappers and mountain men learned how to construct the boats from Plains tribes. It took practice to learn how to climb in and out of a loaded boat, as well as how to paddle the craft or tow it behind a horse. Once the sailor reached dry land, he repacked his horses and was on his way.

A caravan had too much cargo for a bull boat, so crossing rivers became a challenge. Riding and packhorses could swim across if the river was not high or swift. On the Missouri Trail, caravans could find ferry services along the river. These ferries were not boats but large rafts set on dugout canoes or even keelboats. A wagon and horses rode up onto the ferry, and as men hauled on poles and followed currents, the ferry crossed the river. The farther west, the fewer the ferries. Once over the Missouri River at Westport, caravans forded rivers and streams at shallow places.

James Beckwourth was born a slave, freed by his British father, and apprenticed to a blacksmith in St. Louis. He ran away to become a fur trapper, explorer, and adventurer. Although he did not trade regularly in Santa Fe, he was known by many of the Missouri traders and was respected as a guide and a storyteller. (State Historical Society of Missouri, Columbia)

Crossing a river was the least of the men's problems. Lack of food for animals, severe weather, and bad judgment were also deadly. Sometimes both men and animals simply ran out of food. Cottonwood bark fed the animals. Even the men could slice, boil, and eat the soft inner wood of a cottonwood tree when nothing else was available, although often this killed the tree. Alphonso Wetmore recalled trappers he met along the Kansas River. One man lay dead in the canoe. The others were nearly dead. They explained that as they fought off starvation, they boiled up their moccasins and a deerskin bag. The one man died after the meal. As one trapper explained, the dead man had probably just eaten more of the bag than was good for him.

When traders set out, they did so knowing they would spend at least three months traveling approximately 900 miles from Missouri to Santa Fe. Once they crossed the Missouri River and reached the Kansas plains, the men spent wearying weeks moving eighteen miles a day, hunting, repairing wagons, and protecting the goods and stock from theft and injury. Stampedes were dangerous no matter where they came from. Mules and horses could be spooked. M. M. Marmaduke wrote that in

June 1824, the caravan was encamped on the bank of the Arkansas River one day at noon. Suddenly "a great number of buffaloe came running by the camp, and frightened the horses so that many of them broke off from the encampment at full speed and joined in with the buffaloe in the race." Eventually, the horses were recovered, and Marmaduke said he saw at least "ten or fifteen thousand buffaloe." Wetmore's 1828 caravan avoided being run over by a buffalo stampede when one of the men shot the herd's leader and turned aside the galloping animals.

The Missouri Trail was composed of several traces and tracks, and the Santa Fe Trail added alternative routes as the years went on. William Becknell had shown that caravans could travel north, through the Raton Pass, or in a more southerly direction across the sand hills area of Oklahoma. The pass meant hauling mules, horses, and, later, wagons over narrow, rocky, and dangerous paths. The southern route known as the "Cimarron Cut Off" lacked mountains, but it meant harsh travel through the dreaded *jornada*. Alphonso Wetmore ordered his men to fill water barrels sufficient for three days, but in a report to Congress he noted the caravan found water at 3, 4, and 12 miles. M. M. Marmaduke reported that the men traveled for twelve hours and were near exhaustion and collapse from thirst (a dog with the caravan died). "I never in my life," he wrote, "experienced a time when such general alarm and consternation pervaded every person on account of the want of water." But the caravan that most suffered from the lack of water was that of Benjamin Cooper in 1823. Severe thirst caused some men to collapse, and others to drink the filthy water of buffalo wallows and the blood of a buffalo in order to survive.

Once Missourians arrived in Santa Fe, paid duties on their goods, and received permission to trade, they sometimes headed south into Mexico, where the market was less competitive. Some men stayed in Santa Fe throughout the winter; others left for home by early autumn to avoid winter storms on the prairies. Men on the Santa Fe Trail were far from their Missouri homes where families waited, not knowing whether the traders were safe or even alive. Surviving letters show that the men sent mail whenever possible, sometimes with other traders who were leaving sooner for home or with military men who might return to St. Louis or the upper Missouri forts. The letters were passed along with the hope that they would arrive at a distant home post office.

Romulus Culver, described as a "small, spare man with red or sandy hair" wrote to his wife, Mary Ann, in 1845 as he made his way to Santa Fe and the village of Las Vegas. Culver was a civilian from a Weston, Missouri, farm who worked for the United States purchasing corn for the troops. His letters home contained advice for running the household and directions that Mary should kiss the children for him. He thought little of Santa Fe and noted that there were no American women in the town, the only one having died in January 1846. Only a few months after he arrived in New Mexico and just days before he planned to return home, Culver was killed in an uprising. Mary received a letter from Jesse Morris, a friend of the family: "I have a moment only," it read, "to announce to you the melancholy news of the death of your beloved husband and my friend. He was murdered by the Mexicans about twenty days since at Moro." Culver had been killed in an uprising in which several other men died; he was buried in a wagon box on the square in Las Vegas. Mary Culver continued to raise her children on the Missouri farm until the Civil War. Her son later became a judge in Jackson County.

CHAPTER 4

Wagons and Merchandise
on the Missouri Trail

⎯⎯⎯⎯⎯✺⎯⎯⎯⎯⎯

MEXICO WAS RIPE FOR TRADE long before Missouri traders began to trudge into Santa Fe with packsaddles and hope.
Spain had forced generations of New Mexicans to trade only
within Spanish-held territories and, particularly, with the southern
Mexican provinces. But these provinces lay a thousand miles and more
from Santa Fe, and the trip south and back on wooden-wheeled carts
took over a year to complete. The Spanish governors lived in southern
Mexico and had little interest in trade with the northern area called New
Mexico: it was neither profitable nor convenient to reach. The result was
that few regular trading parties went north to Santa Fe, and Santa Feans
could wait more than two years to purchase any but the most basic items.
Goods that finally arrived on the carts were often of poor quality and
outdated. In addition to choking trade, Spain also discouraged attempts
at modernization or manufacturing in cities, which resulted in most
New Mexicans surviving as poor farmers or small shopkeepers with few
chances to change their lives.

So when the 1821 revolution succeeded, New Mexicans greeted the
first Missouri caravan with silver and smiles. Mexico had won its independence from Spain that same year, and the markets were wide open.
William Becknell's timing was perfect. Becknell later told Nathaniel
Patten, "After crossing a mountain country, we arrived at Santa Fe and
were received with apparent pleasure and joy . . . The day after my arrival
I accepted an invitation to visit the Governor . . . whom I found to be

This view of the adobe parish church in Santa Fe also shows the *carrete,* or wooden carts, which had been used for more than a century to bring goods from southern to northern Mexico. Santa Fe traders from America introduced large wagons to the trade. Although many American traders commented derisively on the sun-dried mud and straw brick (adobe) buildings, adobe homes were cool in summer, warm in winter, relatively simple to construct, and available to any family with a shovel, a strong back, and time. (State Historical Society of Missouri, Columbia)

well informed and gentlemanly in manners; his demeanor was courteous and friendly." The governor assured Becknell that trade with Mexico was now possible, and that Americans were welcome to move to Santa Fe and become citizens. But new trading partnerships did not always mean easy friendships. New Mexico was a poor country with roots in an ancient culture. For Americans, the Mexicans represented an exotic culture that had little in common with Missouri life. Upon seeing the adobe buildings of Santa Fe, many traders were shocked at the simple structures, saying they resembled bake ovens or hovels. They thought the town dirty, the people simple. Alphonso Wetmore captured the attitudes of a New Englander and Missourian who traveled with his caravan:

> "Now, Mike," said Sam Larkin, "what would you have taken that town of Santa Fe for, if you never knowed it was a town?"
> "A right smart sprinkle of brick kilns, walled up with earth and flat

roofs, ready for burning . . . The Governor himself lives in a house I wouldn't give my double cabins for."

Of course, many of the traders lived in log buildings with the bark still on the wood, but as Wetmore noted, homesick travelers in a strange land view everything with "uncharitable scrutiny."

Miles M. Marmaduke wrote in 1825 that Mexicans were "friendly" and "quite happy and contented." Some were very wealthy. But according to Marmaduke, they were under the yoke of their priests, practiced "odd" religious ceremonies, and were "entirely destitute of correct moral principles." American "moral principles" did not easily adapt to the more relaxed culture of New Mexico. Here were people who enjoyed their fandangos, public dances where all ages and ranks visited and danced with one another. Women did not wear corsets or anything like the layers of chemise, petticoat, and gown common in St. Louis. Marmaduke and others were especially shocked by the women who smoked in public, wore shorter colorful skirts and blouses, and chatted with men not their husbands. But some Missourians had broader views. Kit Carson, who married Mexican and Indian women, raised his children in both worlds. After his first wife, Singing Grass, an Arapaho, died, Kit brought their daughter Adaline to Franklin where his niece took in the girl until she finished school. The trader McKnight remained in Santa Fe after his release from prison, married a Mexican woman, and took Mexican citizenship.

Alphonso Wetmore seemed more accepting of the differences between Mexico and Missouri, although he still displayed the sense of superiority common among Western emigrants. His servant on the Santa Fe Trail was a Mexican who was called "the Corporal" and was a buffalo hunter. But despite the Corporal's skills, Wetmore wrote of the man as a servant who possessed little more than broken English. Still, the servant proved himself a worthy member of the caravan: during a buffalo hunt, "a furious old bull, turned on his pursuer and the Corporal threw himself from the saddle and spread his blanket over the head of his assailant, which so effectually blinded him that he was easily dispatched." Later, two of Wetmore's friends told the Mexicans Wetmore was the cousin of Andrew Jackson. The men were so impressed "a grand *fandango* was given the distinguished stranger, at which . . . [Wetmore and his friends] . . . alternately

Many photographs and drawings exist of Christopher "Kit" Carson as an adult. Carson was depicted in magazines and novels as an adventurous hero, but in real life Kit was self-effacing and quiet. Here, he is shown after gaining fame as John Fremont's guide. (State Historical Society of Missouri, Columbia)

danced with the wife and daughter of the civil governor." But as much as the Americans disapproved of their new customers, most accepted the hospitality of the residents, and few traders left Mexico without trying to make a profit.

To do that, the men needed goods to trade and wagons to move the goods. The first traders down the Missouri and Santa Fe Trails used their own horses to pack or pull the goods and owned both the animals and the merchandise they took. By 1824, mules joined the trade and in 1829, oxen first ambled along the trail. Although pack animals made trade possible, they did not make travel simple. Pack animals had to be unloaded at night, then repacked in the morning, a complicated process when the train had one hundred animals or more. A line of pack horses or mules required food, water, and equipment, and as the numbers of animals grew, so did the traders' problems. Grains and forage were carried along in wagons or the animals were tied out and allowed to graze along the trail. But in addition to food and water, each animal required leather "tack," including reins, harnesses, and saddles. The equipment was expensive: men who could not afford a "rig" as a trader hired out as drivers to those who could. Many Missouri traders were hired to manage other men's trade as the demand for goods increased.

William Becknell had discovered in 1821 that the Raton Pass into Santa Fe was dangerous for horses and all but impossible for wagons. Perhaps he spoke with trappers who were in Santa Fe and knew the region, or Ezekiel Williams offered advice about New Mexico. Whatever the reason, when Becknell left Santa Fe to return to Missouri, he followed a trail that avoided the mountains and took less travel time. Becknell recognized that wagons could transport more than any string of packhorses, and he meant to be the first wagon master.

What types of wagons creaked out of Franklin in spring 1822? Light farm wagons were probably most easily acquired, as were carriages, including a "Dearborn," named after its inventor. This lightweight carriage was not suitable for carrying trade goods, although it had drop-down curtains so it may have provided more comfort and protection from rain and wind than open wagons. In addition, there was little room for merchandise and the carriages often broke down from the rattling and pounding of trail travel that sometimes destroyed wagons as well. Alphonso Wetmore wrote that on his 1828 Santa Fe journey, "We discovered the corpse of a wagon which had been left by the preceding caravan. O Temperance! O Ditch Water!" But any conveyance that arrived in Santa Fe benefitted traders: Becknell paid $150 for his wagon in Missouri and sold it in Mexico for $700. That kind of profit encouraged traders to abandon pack trains for wagons.

The Santa Fe Trail wagons have become ghosts; as far as is known, no complete, original wagon exists. While farm wagons were the first wheeled vehicles to go west, the wagon most frequently identified with the trail was the Conestoga wagon. Missouri farm wagons had flat beds, lighter construction, and were lower to the ground than the Conestoga wagon. The Conestoga—for the Conestoga region Pennsylvania—may have also started life as a farm wagon. It is mentioned as early as the eighteenth century. But the Conestoga wagons adapted to the needs of trade and trails: the rear wheels became larger to pass over stumps and rocks, and a cover

Covered wagons descended from the sturdy farm wagons of Pennsylvania. This drawing shows a Missouri-built wagon used in the Santa Fe trade. The boat-shaped "bed" shows why the vehicles were called prairie "schooners," after the masted sailing ships. This wagon is missing the hoops that held up the white canvas cover. (State Historical Society of Missouri, Columbia)

was pulled over a wooden frame to protect trade goods. As roads were cleared and widened, the wagons followed suit, growing in height and width, increasing the amount of goods they could transport. Conestoga wagon makers were masters at using different types of wood, including oak, hickory, poplar, and black gum for the axle, wheels, and wagon box, or body. The proper selection of wood could mean the difference between a wagon that rumbled and creaked for hundreds of uneventful miles or one that broke down frequently. Fastened to the wagon sides and bent above the wagon bed were a series of hoops called bows. These supported the "Osnaburg" covers (a heavy linen or cotton canvas, also used for ships' sails), which gave "covered wagons" their name. The fabric came from Osnabrueck, Germany, a center for linen trade and production.

Covered wagons were colorful, with red painted wheels and woodwork, blue or green bodies, and white canvas. S. Wilson wrote of "white covers glistening in the sun," while another writer declared the wagons resembled "posey baskets on wheels." Some wagon owners painted names on their vehicles. Missouri wagons carried kegs of water, a side box that served as a feedbox for the animals, and a pot or bucket of pine tar and resin for greasing the wheels. (Without the grease to reduce friction, axles could burst into flame and destroy the entire wagon and contents.) Some wagon drivers attached strings of bells to the harness. The bells were a matter of pride: to "arrive with bells on" meant a driver was ready for some fun. Any wagon driver whose wagon got stuck in mud or quicksand depended upon another driver to help pull him out, but he had to surrender the bells to the rescuer. Another piece of trail "equipment" was a large, cheap cigar, known as a "stogie" and named after the Conestoga wagon.

It is not clear who built the "first" Conestoga wagon for the Missouri trail. Santa Fe traders had several ways to obtain wagons. Wealthy men purchased wagons in Pennsylvania and shipped them by river to Missouri. Others bought their wagons locally. St. Louis was home to wagonmakers as were Franklin and Boonville. Hiram Young was in business in Independence by 1851, and by 1860 was employing as many as twenty men and making between eight and nine hundred wagons a year.

The Conestogas were practical and well built for trade. The wagon beds curved upwards like a ship at either end, resulting in a center lower than its ends. This kept the goods from shifting back and forth as the wagon went up and down hills. Pittsburgh wagons were said to be larger and heavier than the Conestoga, and described by one trader as "cumbersome affairs with long deep beds. A man 6 feet tall could stand erect in one of them."

A third type of wagon was made by Joseph Murphy of St. Louis. Murphy reportedly constructed the largest wagons to cross Missouri for Santa Fe. Legend said the Murphy wagon tongue was fifty feet long and the tires double the width of any other. A giant indeed: some said the wagons could carry 7,000 pounds of goods. But despite this frontier boast, there is little proof that Murphy wagons were much different from other Santa Fe vehicles. As Mexican traders began to make the journey from Santa Fe to St. Louis some Americans admired the elaborate wagons from Santa Fe. They seem to have been fitted up like modern rail cars, with sleeping accommodations for women who accompanied their husbands. But Americans preferred to use their wagon space for commerce, not comfort.

Wagons for the trade carried heavy loads and survived thousands of miles on the road. Americans were proud of the vehicles, as noted in the *Niles Weekly Register* in 1834:

[German] wagons compared with ours, for strength . . . and fitness or *accommodation* for long journeys over the mountains and other rough parts of our roads, are as pigmies standing by the side of giants. . . . [Ours] are often loaded with from three to four tons—and being well covered, effectually protect persons and property from many of the inclemencies of the season—and they are so capacious that we have frequently seen as many as twenty persons, women and children, comfortably stowed over their own packages of goods . . . The American "Conestoga wagon," has been often figuratively called a "land ship." It is fitted for its business.

But as dependable as the wagons were on land, they were not very river-worthy. Wagons had to cross streams and rivers without sinking or flipping over, miring in quicksand, or dumping the goods into the current. If a river wasn't too deep, the wagon boxes might be caulked inside with tar, covered with buffalo skins outside and floated over. At least one driver, caught on the plains in winter, packed the crevices in his wagon box with snow, wet it down with water, and allowed it to freeze, making the box watertight and allowing it to float across the ice-filled river. But whatever the method used, water crossings were costly and time consuming. One trader wrote that ferrying freight for a large wagon train across the Missouri might take a week or more at a cost of $100 a day. A single man with a string of packhorses might cross in a canoe, leading his swimming horses. Mules could swim, but oxen preferred to walk a shallow river ford. Animals might be loaded onto rafts and taken across, but when there were hundreds of mules, the water crossings seemed endless.

Back on the trails, the guide—known as a muleteer or bullwhacker, depending upon whether mules or oxen were in the caravan—walked alongside or rode the animal closest to the front left wheel. According to accounts, certain wagons had a plank board that extended from the side, creating a riding seat called the "lazy board." But for the most part, only the ill or infirm rode. On the Missouri Trail, the men walked.

As Missouri sent more merchandise to the southwest, the power for moving the goods had to increase as well. Horses were limited to the amount of goods they could carry—perhaps 300 pounds apiece—they were fast, but not the best animals for packing goods. The first horses down the trail and across Missouri needed good grass and water, neither of which was always available. Some traders took along a wagon filled

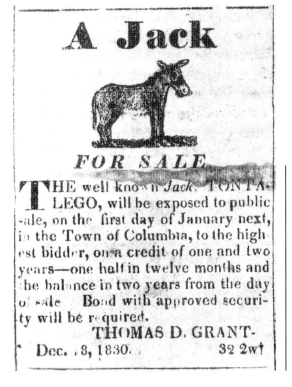

A Jack

FOR SALE.

THE well known *Jack*, TONTA-LEGO, will be exposed to public sale, on the first day of January next, in the Town of Columbia, to the highest bidder, on a credit of one and two years—one half in twelve months and the balance in two years from the day of sale. Bond with approved security will be required.

THOMAS D. GRANT.

Dec. 8, 1830.   32 2wt

Mules were important to the Santa Fe Trail economy, and Missouri mules became famous around the world. The mule was a cross between a male donkey ("jack") and female horse. Here, Tonta-Lego ("foolish and ignorant"), a jack, is advertised for purchase by auction. (State Historical Society of Missouri, Columbia)

with corn for the horses, and then sold the empty wagon in New Mexico. Horses had sensitive hooves, a problem when climbing rocky paths. They spooked in severe weather and at the noise and movement of Indian raids and stampedes. Horses were fine with light wagons, but the conditions of prairie travel, coupled with the development of heavier freight wagons, meant horses were soon changed out for the stubborn, rough, and smart mule that became available in the trade.

Mules were among the first trade items brought back from Mexico, where the tough little animals survived poor food, hard use, and rough terrain. Mules were farm animals accustomed to difficult work and long days. A cross between a jackass (a male donkey) and a mare (female horse), the mule was known for its stamina and strength. It could survive the desert crossings better than horses, needing to drink only the water it had lost. Mules had tougher hides that withstood the extremes of weather (and of a muleskinner's whip). They were easier to shoe than horses and had better hooves for rough terrain, an important consideration on the trail. Mules were known, if not always appreciated, for their independent attitude and quick intelligence and were excellent at self-preservation. A horse might jump a ditch and hurt a leg; a mule thought its way safely around.

Mules were hitched in pairs. Each wagon hitch included leaders (the animals at the front), the swing and off-side swing leaders (second in line from the front), and the near wheeler (left side) and off-side wheeler (right). The leaders showed the mule team where and how to move. Mules were guided by a single jerk line held by the muleteer. This line had to be held at a certain angle, which was not possible if the muleteer rode in the wagon. Instead, he walked alongside or rode the near wheeler, which also allowed him to crack his whip without hitting the wagon. Once Missourians saw the Mexican mule—a light and small animal—they brought tens of thousands back up the trail to sell down South and throughout Missouri as farm animals. But others bred a larger, stronger mule for the freighters: the Missouri mule, which became legendary for its power and personality.

Mules in general were known for their ability to run far and long, and when mules ran off with a wagon or a pack, it was often simpler to let them go until they tired out. Alphonso Wetmore told a typical mule story about his own experiences, using the fictional name of Rainmore:

> After passing the Semiron, the buffalo were so abundant that those who had a taste for field sports, could scarcely be restrained from indulgence in it. . . . Even Captain Rainmore . . . galloped his mule in chase of some of the fattest. Drawing a pistol [he fired, but] . . . , the obstinate animal which he rode threw up his head and received the shot. The animal fell and left the rider on foot.

Wetmore was upset over the loss of his mule, but without much choice he began the walk back to camp. Suddenly, the "mule rose sufficiently recovered to follow him back to the columns of the Caravan. The ball had flattened on the hard head of the ass-colt, and he was entirely well ten days afterwards."

A Missouri trader who drove mules was called a muleskinner for his skill with a whip. The long whip was used to get the mules' attention with a cracking sound: a good muleskinner didn't strike the mule and had to be smarter than his four-legged assistant. A mule would bite, kick, buck, and sit down. He would take a deep breath when the harness was cinched around him and then let out the air, letting the straps go loose and the pack swing under the mule and drop the carefully packed trade goods to the ground. A greenhorn (an inexperienced trader) would watch helplessly as his mule threw off its pack and trampled happily over the goods.

People believed that mules respected a man who could holler and curse a blue streak, and Missourians became famous for their colorful language and intricate curses. According to one story, Indians listened to the traders' language, and from that, they learned to call oxen "whoa-haws" and wagons "goddams." At least one freighting company tried to improve the culture of the trail. Men who signed on as a wagoneer, muleskinner, or bullwhacker received a Bible and signed a contract that said, "While I am in the employ of Majors, Russell and Waddell, I am not to use profane language, not to get drunk, not to gamble, not to treat animals cruelly, not to do anything else that is incompatible with the conduct of a gentleman and I agree if I violate any of the above conditions to accept my discharge without collecting any pay for my services." It is not known whether the mules agreed to the contract.

The third animal used to draw wagons was the ox. The heavy, slow, patient, and good-natured ox had worked American farms since the seventeenth century, but few men thought the animals were suited for a journey to Santa Fe. Then in 1829, Major Bennett Riley was sent with troops as a military guard for the Santa Fe traders. Riley had to bring along equipment and supplies and he didn't want a pack train spread across the plains. Instead, he decided to see whether oxen could pull heavier wagons with more trade goods. In addition to hauling up to 7,000 pounds per wagon, fewer oxen were needed per wagon than mules. This would result in larger profits, and would make up for the slower pace of the animals when compared with mules. Riley thought that oxen were cheaper than mules—a team of six oxen cost about the same as two mules, and one ox team could haul nearly double the weight hauled by mules. One drawback was that oxen stampeded easily at the sight of snakes or, as one bullwhacker found out, a coat. The man had tracked a stray ox and was leading it back to the caravan. The day being warm, the bullwhacker had thrown his coat over the animal's horns. As man and animal got closer

A well-organized caravan traveled in parallel lines, which allowed the wagons to "square up," forming an enclosed space for men and stock, or circle into a protective ring. The protection was not only needed against harassment from unfriendly Indians or robbers but from weather: when the conditions were right for a "devil wind" (a tornado), caravans might dig ditches and drive the wagons into the ditches, then chain the wagons together for greater protection. This train has mules as well as oxen. (State Historical Society of Missouri, Columbia)

to the wagons, the ox trotted ahead with the coat flapping in the breeze, sending the rest of the oxen into a frightened mad dash across the prairie.

Once on the trail, problems with the oxen grew more complicated. River crossings were difficult, since the animals and wagons easily bogged down in sand and quicksand. Some wagons needed more than a dozen pair of oxen to get free, which took a lot of time and hard work. (Oxen weren't the only animals to bog down. Josiah Gregg told of having to haul mules out of quicksand by their ears.) Major Riley complained in a report that his progress was slower because the oxen were "of different ages, some old and some young and not used to be put together and the teamsters not accustomed to drive them." The animals tired more easily than mules on the plains. Riley tried to be fair, and wrote that the oxen tired easily because they were kept yoked and tied to wagon wheels out of fear the animals would stray or be stolen. Riley's worries were confirmed when an Indian raid resulted in the loss of fifty-four oxen. Eventually, raiders realized that oxen were less valuable than mules and horses, and fewer oxen were stolen. "Corn freight" was used to describe a shipment drawn by mules and horses, who needed the grains to eat. This was a faster shipping method than "hay freight" or oxen, but corn freight was also more expensive.

Mules and horses were smarter than oxen and had to be watched carefully on the trail. But oxen followed their leader. Each pair was yoked, and a sensible bullwhacker always yoked a wild and a lazy ox—two easygoing animals meant a slow and dragging outfit. The "wheelers" (the oxen closest to the wagon) were large animals who acted as brakes, slowing down the wagon if they felt it starting to move too fast. Once the pairs were used to working together, the bullwhacker marked his animals to make it easier to find them in the corral. (Corrals were formed by chaining wagons together and driving animals into the center space.) Josiah Gregg wrote that despite these precautions, "the oxen soon burst their way out, and though mostly yoked in pairs they went scampering over the plains . . . it would require Auld Clootie himself [a Scottish name for the devil] to check the headway of . . . oxen when thoroughly frightened."

Mules, horses, and oxen all wore metal "shoes" that required the services of a blacksmith. Sometimes reshoeing was managed on the trails, but few inexperienced men wanted to shoe a mule, and oxen were too heavy and dangerous to lift without a hoist. In a few cases, when an ox threw or lost a shoe, he was fitted with buffalo skin "moccasins" to cushion the hooves. Mules, however, were left to fend for themselves. Once they lost their shoes, a mule's hooves were smoothed down by use, and on a wet, grassy prairie, the animals would slip and slide as if on a frozen river.

Muleskinners rode the "nigh-wheeler" mule and used a "blacksnake" whip. The whip was long enough to reach the backs of balky mules, but not long enough to hit the top of the wagon when snapped. The bullwhacker walked along by the nigh-wheeler ox. Since he did not have to worry about hitting the top of the wagon, the bullwhacker's whip was up to twenty feet or longer and had leather pieces called "poppers" or "crackers" attached to the end. This is what made the famous cracking sound when the whip was snapped. Most muleskinners and bullwhackers used the sound to urge on the animals and struck an animal only in dangerous circumstances. The men were experts with the whips, and kept in practice by snapping the heads off rattlesnakes, knocking coins off sticks, or snapping another man's jeans to shreds while he was still in them. In the later days of the trail, the wagon masters (trail leaders) and freighters (traders and workers) were French Canadian, Welsh, Scots, Italian, German, Irish, English, black, Shawnee, and Cherokee. Whoever could take life on the trail was welcomed, but at least one man recalled that "the prominent, noticeable, rollicking dare-devils" came, for the most part, from Missouri.

The people of the Missouri-Kansas border were used to all the odd sights of a western caravan but certainly the strangest sight arrived in 1846. That was the first time a Missouri newspaper mentioned a wind wagon, the brainchild of William Thomas, a dreamer and adventurer. In December 1846, the *Independence Expositor* announced: "The Wind Wagon Works. Mr. Thomas ran up and down the plains with his wagon at pleasure. It is his intention to move his family to Independence and with a partner (an old tar) begin a shipping business 'to Santa Fe in a reasonable time at $6 per hundred pounds.'" According to the article, Thomas hoped to create a transcontinental wind wagon service with "cars" on both sides of rivers, ready to sweep across the prairies to California and Santa Fe.

The idea of using wind to push a land vehicle was not new: as early as the sixteenth century, travelers wrote of Chinese "land ships," or sailing wagons, which moved overland through a combination of wind and canvas sails, and Dutch artists depicted wind wagons on pottery and china. How the idea for a wind wagon came west is not known, but as early as 1846, "Mr. Thomas" was at work developing a wind wagon somewhere near Independence. The *Independence Expositor* described the vehicle in detail:

> The construction of the wagon is very simple. It is a frame made of plank, well braced and placed edgewise on four axle-trees, four wheels to each side, these wheels to be 12 feet or more in diameter and one foot broad. . . . Two tongues are joined together forward of the wagon and by ropes coming to the wheel similar to the pilot wheel of the a steamboat, the wagon is steered by a pilot. The sails are like to the sails and rigging of a ship . . . Mr. Thomas expects to convey freight and passengers . . . to Santa Fe.

By 1853, Thomas had founded the Overland Navigation Company and convinced several merchants to invest in his dream. No one is certain where the wind wagon was built: some historians say the Foundry and Brass Works in Independence made the wagon. Others claim that Fritz Lauber of Westport was the builder. The wind wagon was like nothing else seen on the prairie. The large wheels lifted the wagon bed over any obstacles. Thomas had the contraption shipped across the Missouri River and towed out to the Kansas prairie, accompanied by curious townspeople and the investors. The wind wagon caught at the breeze, then took off across the grassland bumping and rocking and gathering speed. Finally, it hit a waterless stream bed and was wrecked, along with the dreams of Thomas, who did not make it to New Mexico.

But a fortune awaited anyone who could make the trip to Santa Fe faster and more comfortable. Thomas was discouraged, but several others tried their hand at building a successful wind wagon. August Rodert and John Parker were competitors in the wind wagon race. Rodert's wind wagon used a small windmill to power the vehicle. Parker designed and built a wagon with a mast and four crossarms. The front and rear axles were steered separately by men who stood in the wagon. It was a large vehicle, at least twenty feet in length and four feet wide, and brightly painted. According to one story, Parker's wagon was pulled to the prairie by oxen (mules refused to go near it). The wagon was left there overnight and in the morning was gone. It was never found, and folks believed it was sailing the prairies under its own steam.

Perhaps the most successful wind wagon captain was Samuel Peppard. He built a wind wagon in the 1860s that traveled fast enough to pass emigrant wagons on the way to Pike's Peak. A newspaperman writing for *Leslie's Illustrated Magazine* described it:

> The Wind Ship of the Prairies: Fort Kearney, May 27, 1860. The prairie ship, . . . is a very light built wagon, the body rounded in front, something in shape like a boat. The wheels are remarkably light, large and slender, and the whole vehicle strongly built. Two masts . . . carry large square sails, rigged like a ship's. . . . In front is a large coach lamp, to travel by night when the wind is favorable. . . . The ship hove in sight about eight o'clock in the morning, with a fresh breeze from N.E. by E.; it was running down in a westerly direction for the fort, under full sail across the green prairie. The guard, astonished at such a novel sight, reported the matter to the officer on duty, and we all turned out to view the phenomenon.

Although wind wagons were used in China centuries ago, the idea of using the prairie winds to propel a vehicle did not gain ground until the 1840s. There were several wind wagon designs, from a plank-wide seat with sails and wheels to a full-sized wagon, capable of carrying folks across the prairies in comfort. (State Historical Society of Missouri, Columbia)

Outside of Denver the wagon was picked up by a "whirlwind" and dropped to the ground. (Other stories were less dramatic, reporting that the wind wagon blew into a ravine and was smashed to bits.) Peppard survived, continued his trip with friends, and told of the adventure for many years, but as far as is known, a wind wagon never arrived in Santa Fe.

The Santa Fe trade was powered by merchandise—every man, mule, horse, and ox that trudged down to Santa Fe and back again to Missouri did so because of goods to be sold or bought. Trade meant money to a state short of gold and silver, and from the start, the Santa Fe trade was lucrative. William Becknell warned those who came after him, "Those who visit the country for the purpose of vending merchandise will do well to take goods of excellent quality and unfaded colors. . . . money and mules are plentiful, and [the Santa Feans] do not hesitate to pay the price demanded for an article if it suits their purpose." New Mexicans were no longer satisfied with cheap and poorly made goods. Missouri traders carried brightly colored cotton fabrics, clothing, woolen yard goods, jewelry, sewing pins, and hand mirrors. In later years, other items, including beer and gold-mining machinery, were freighted across the plains, along with weapons, food, and clothing for the American military. Missouri men made a profit both west and east, taking goods to Santa Fe and bringing back mules, jacks and jennets, and, later, raw wool, lead, and minerals. Some traders even sold their worn-out trail animals and wagons. Since the average cost in 1843 for a new wagon, mules, and equipment was $1,300, the Santa Fe trade was indeed profitable even with secondhand equipment.

As the trail's business increased, so did the amount of goods. James Josiah Webb, was a New Englander who entered the trade at St. Louis. In his memoirs about trail days, Webb listed goods purchased for trade including fabrics such as linen and striped cloth, sheeting, cambric, fine French lawn, alpaca, bandanas, Irish linen, shawls, shirts, hosiery, ties, gloves, and suspenders. Gold rings, ivory combs, and necklaces were included for the ladies. Some goods contributed to the trail's vocabulary. "Looking glasses" were small mirrors and a "looking glass prairie" was a wetlands area that reflected light and created mirages. Even such large and heavy items as log chains, shovels, axes, and irons were packed up and taken west to New Mexican markets. This meant cotton growers in the southern United States had large new markets to supply. Cotton was more than cloth to the trail—it was the symbol of American domestic manufacture, an important issue for politicians and traders. The Santa Fe trade was not a simple exchange of goods between Missouri and New Mexico but an intricate web of supply and demand, manufacture and politics. The growers not only wanted this business, they wanted to choke out the import of cotton from Europe.

The earliest Santa Fe trade was based upon cotton goods and other items purchased in the Boonslick, carted across the plains, and sold in Mexico. Becknell had believed that an initial investment in merchandise of $300 ($10 per thirty men) would do for the first trip to Santa Fe. But within a few years, caravans were hauling goods worth hundreds of thousands of dollars between Missouri and New Mexico. Traders could expect a profit of anywhere from 25 to 100 percent, and there were years when nearly a million dollars changed hands between traders and Mexican buyers. Alphonso Wetmore wrote to Congress in 1825 that profits of 300 percent were common, especially when beaver pelts, mules, and silver were the trade goods. Despite the enormous profits that could be realized, it took a few years for traders to realize that a trip to the wholesalers—and not to local middlemen—would make them even more of a profit. Missouri merchants were not wholesalers and their prices were high, so high that in the early days of the trail, a trader realized he could still ship his goods from the East and make a profit in Santa Fe.

Traders made a trip back East to Philadelphia and New York in the autumn, chose their goods, and had them shipped to the Boonslick by the spring, when they would set out over the Plains for Santa Fe. The trade—although referred to as the Southwest or Western trade—had international connections. Pittsburgh offered cheap metal goods, Kentucky provided whiskey and paper, New York boasted European wares, including printed cottons. By the 1830s, Missourians were acting as agents for Eastern merchants. St. Louis became a destination for American traders buying goods and heading west and for Mexican merchants bringing goods for sale in the East. Robert Aull began as a merchant in Franklin, and then started the first "chain" of stores west of the Mississippi River. Men like St. Louis trader James Webb had an additional advantage over early traders like Becknell: Webb shipped his goods from St. Louis to Westport in relative safety on a steamboat.

Getting the goods to Santa Fe was difficult, but American merchants faced even greater problems once they entered New Mexico. Like Missouri, New Mexico had a new government. It had circulating money, but much of it was leaving the country in traders' pockets. The Santa Fe trade meant a new source for merchandise and import duties. In order to do business in New Mexico, traders paid a tax based upon the number and types of goods imported. And, of course, Missourians complained about overcharges and unfair duties and tried to fight back. Smuggling was managed by layering blankets in between the wagon covers—which also kept the goods inside the wagon dry. Since only wagons with goods were taxed upon entering New Mexico, Missourians began stopping outside of Santa Fe after the worst of the trip was over. They loaded as much of their goods as possible onto one wagon, and drove the empty wagons into the town to sell. There the traders faced oftentimes corrupt inspectors who examined the goods and could withhold a "commercial passport" or *guia* from the traders unless a bribe was paid.

Duties were paid at the custom house upon entering Mexico; if papers were not correct, the shipment could be seized at any time. The bills and documents had to be written in Spanish and prove absolutely accurate or fines were set and goods seized. Since the rules were not consistent, traders who headed south out of Santa Fe faced the same trials over and over. Officials required bribes, and there was a 20 percent internal tax on the goods. Domestic manufactured goods were taxed once, but imported goods were taxed twice: upon entering the United States and then in Mexico. Americans were enraged that they were taxed by their own country when they imported goods for the Santa Fe trade and then taxed again in Santa Fe. American fabrics were heavier and of better quality than English calicoes and cottons, but English goods were often cheaper, and traders preferred to purchase those over others produced in America. And if this was not enough, Americans had to apply for and hold a passport, which was not accepted everywhere in the country. Josiah Gregg told of men who were threatened with jail, blackmailed, fined, thrown into prison or held until it was wintertime and dangerous to cross the plains. Missourians complained loudly, asking their Senator Thomas Benton to intercede.

The trade to Missouri was not one way, and Mexicans quickly became skilled traders and businessmen. They traveled west to east, purchasing goods for their own country and trading blankets, furs, silver, mules and other items with merchants from Westport to St. Louis. Across the state, Mexican traders were familiar sights, from Weston to Boonslick to the Mississippi River. By the 1850s, Mexican traders were responsible for nearly half the Santa Fe Trail trade, and were as common a sight in Independence and Westport as any American trader. Alphonso Wetmore wrote that he entertained a friend from Mexico at his home in Franklin. The Mexicans traveled farther east—to New York, Baltimore, and Pennsylvania—to order goods from wholesalers for shipment home as well as to arrange for the import and export of goods from overseas. Some Mexican traders sent their children to schools in St. Louis, especially those run by nuns of the Catholic Church, which was a powerful force in Mexico.

The taxation problem in New Mexico caused both American and Hispanic traders to rethink their businesses. Mexico did not have a consistent method for taxing imports and exports, and therefore traders paid extremely high taxes on goods and wagons. Bribery sometimes worked, but Missouri traders risked imprisonment and heavy fines if they failed to

Meredith Miles Marmaduke served as Missouri's eighth governor, completing the term of Governor Thomas Reynolds. He also took an active role in the Santa Fe trade, leading caravans and successfully importing goods between Mexico and the United States. He lived in Franklin and was an acquaintance of Alphonso Wetmore. Marmaduke was a son-in-law of Dr. John Sappington. This portrait reveals Marmaduke as a bit of a dandy. (State Historical Society of Missouri, Columbia)

declare their goods and pay the tax. Senator Benton tried to start negotiations between the United States and Mexico in order to reduce or at least control the tax problems, but little success came of his attempts. Joseph Murphy reportedly built his enormous wagons so that traders could carry more in one load and not have to pay for several vehicles. Despite taxes, however, the profits realized on some trade goods were worth the trouble. John Turley, a Missouri trader, reported that in 1825 he bought whiskey for 16 to 40¢ a gallon in Franklin and sold it in Taos for $3 a gallon—after watering it down. "It was terrible stuff, too," he recalled.

Missourians tried to protect their rights to the trade. As early as 1824, Missouri traders wrote to local newspapers, warning traders that business in Mexico was done. They reported a glut on the market, too many goods and not enough silver. That some of this was true was indicated by letters and reports from men including Alphonso Wetmore and M. Miles Marmaduke who complained that they had to travel into southern Mexico in order to unload their goods. But there seemed to be enough trade to encourage new and larger caravans each year. At least one Missouri newspaperman wrote that those who had the interests of Missouri at heart would not broadcast the value of the Santa Fe trade, so that other states would stay away and leave the best deals to Missourians, who, after all, "were the first to explore the route and find the market, and in our opinion, ought to reap the advantages resulting from the discovery."

CHAPTER 5

The F-A-R W-E-S-T

Missouri Trail Towns

———— ⟨⟨⟨⟩ ————

T HE SANTA FE TRAIL WAS never a single trace, track, or path. Men and wagons, like water, find their own levels and directions. Like the Missouri River, the trail had cutoffs, braids, and alternate routes. Arrow Rock could be reached by traveling west across the prairie from Franklin or by crossing the river at Boonville and then heading west. Traders might go to Lexington and then on to Independence or head to Fort Osage. As towns and villages waxed and waned, caravans passed through places new and old. Within only a few years after the start of the trail, Franklin had disappeared; the settlement at Arrow Rock had grown, named itself New Philadelphia, then decided to change back to Arrow Rock. Fort Osage was abandoned to the wolves, and Independence was living up to its name as it passed its early years in the woods instead of on the prairie.

But no matter how it changed in shape, the trail always moved west across the state, like a sunflower following its namesake. The Boonslick Trail from St. Charles to Franklin was approximately 130 miles. The rest of the trail, from Franklin to the Missouri River on the western line, was roughly 160 miles: Franklin to Arrow Rock, 24 miles; Arrow Rock to Lexington, 73; Lexington to Fort Osage, 23; Fort Osage to Independence, 17; Independence to Westport, 13 and Westport to New Santa Fe, 11. A good journey by horse across the state might take eleven days or less, but with wagons it took at least three weeks. If there was rain, or ground soaked by storms or streams over their banks, several weeks' travel was common.

Missouri traders set out without maps, guided by what others told them about the best route, the best springs for the stock, the best places to stop and camp. Travel along the Missouri Trail was by gosh, by guess, and by golly in the early days. In later years, after thousands of wagon wheels had bitten into the plains along the trail, travelers followed the paths of those who had gone before. The main stops along the route changed in importance through the years: the trailhead—the town considered by traders to be the start of the trail—moved steadily west, from Franklin, Boonville, Arrow Rock, Fort Osage, Independence, to Westport. Over the years it moved west, reached Westport, and then was no more than a few miles long within the state of Missouri.

This shortening occurred for several reasons. First, the Missouri was a wild river, unconstricted by modern levees and dikes. In the time of the trail, the river could flood the bottomlands, eat up towns, and change the face of the landscape in the blink of a watery eye. At least one town–Franklin—had disappeared into the river, forcing the trail to move west where the river wasn't as ornery and the settlements could be placed on higher ground.

Second, steamboats improved their ability to navigate the Missouri River. The earliest steamboats to reach Franklin arrived in 1819—the commercial ship *Independence* and the *Jefferson,* which was part of a government expedition. (The *Jefferson* was also the first ship to sink in the Missouri River.) The early steamboat pilots quickly discovered that Missouri River mud and sand clogged engines, causing the ships to spin in circles or run aground. Alphonso Wetmore saw the early Missouri steamboats and was not impressed: "This small craft was observed just getting underway. Marvelous as it may seem, some malconstruction of the machinery that was designed to propel the boat worked inversely, and carried her stern-foremost up stream." But within ten years, improvements allowed steamboats to travel upriver to the area that is now Kansas City, and Santa Fe traders could move goods by water to starting points farther west before beginning down the trail.

Within little more than a decade after the War of 1812, the Boonslick had changed from an Indian homeland to a white settlement area. Indian tribes—the Ioway and the Kansas among them—were forced from their ancestral homes, many victims of unfair treaties and broken promises. Tribes were shoved west across the Missouri and held in check through military strength, meaningless peace agreements, destruction of camping areas and resources by emigrants, and new illnesses such as measles. This destruction of Indian cultures resulted in increased white settlement and commercial development along the Missouri Trail. Each town along the trail was there because of business: Franklin was a trading center, Arrow Rock offered a good ferry crossing, Fort Osage was a trading post, Independence provided access to fine wagons, ox yokes, and mules. Traders stopped at towns that had the best conditions for beginning a trading trip. As one town offered better services and goods than the last, the trade moved west with the commerce, until, by the 1840s, the Missouri Trail was only a few miles long. Still, each town along the Missouri Trail had its own personality and made its own contribution to Santa Fe Trail history.

Franklin was settled in 1816 by emigrants who had fought the War of 1812 in Missouri. It was the main town in the Boonslick area. Named for Benjamin Franklin, the town grew quickly—from 120 log houses in 1819 to a bustling settlement by 1823. When the painter and scientist Titian Ramsay Peale visited Franklin in 1819, he noted that the town had more than 1,000 people and that 100 had shown up to greet the *Western Engineer* as it steamed by.

Franklin was home to the first U.S. land office west of St. Louis, where settlers could file their claims for land in the new territory. The town itself was not large—less than a mile square, divided into neat blocks and unimproved streets. But Franklin could offer much of what a visitor might find in St. Louis. The town had a road that led from the Missouri River to the public square. The square was surrounded by streets of cabins, a log jail, more than thirteen shops, and professional offices for doctors, lawyers, and teachers. Brick buildings were constructed from the natural clay found along the river. The clay was shaped and baked, or "burned," in kilns, often by slaves. Bricks sold for ten dollars a thousand and uncleared lands cost between two to fifteen dollars an acre. Some houses were of sawn lumber and whitewashed, standing in stark contrast to the grey-brown cabins with mud chinking and stick chimneys.

Franklin was a bustling town as well as the largest western town after St. Louis. Here, a visitor might attend a dance, have a tooth pulled, buy a book, get a watch repaired, have hair and beard trimmed, stop at a hotel for dinner, and, if it happened to be the Fourth of July, enjoy a series of toasts, speeches, and dances in honor of the nation. Nathaniel Patten, Franklinite and the Boonslick's first newspaper editor, offered a toast in 1825 to his adopted home: "Our Own State—destined by nature to become a star of the first magnitude in the constellation of the Union." Patten had a difficult job as editor of the finest newspaper west of the Mississippi, the *Missouri Intelligencer and Boonslick Advertiser.* Times in Franklin were never easy, and Patten often ran announcements begging readers to pay their subscriptions in produce and crops. But thankfully the *Missouri Intelligencer* survived and was the first paper to detail the beginning of the Santa Fe Trail.

Still, Franklin was on the frontier, and a place Reverend John Peck, a traveling minister, described jokingly as "the F-a-r W-e-s-t." But the town was home to educated and ambitious men as well as adventurers and dreamers. Several future governors of Missouri lived in Franklin, as did Christopher "Kit" Carson.

Imagine Henry Vest Bingham's inn, in Franklin, the Square and Compass. A young boy sat and sketched pictures. He watched as keel-boatmen, trappers, traders, Indians, and soldiers met at the hotel to find a fight or dance to a fiddle and a frying pan drum. The boy, George Caleb Bingham, never forgot Franklin. In later years, he gained fame as the "Missouri artist" by bringing friends and neighbors to life in his paintings.

Bingham's inn was home for a time in 1820 to the itinerant artist Chester Harding, whose portraits included those of Army officer Alphonso Wetmore and Daniel Boone. Harding traveled frequently through the Boonslick to paint portraits, and during one return trip to the inn, he was confronted by a huge panther in the road and lived to tell the tale to his grandchildren.

As might be expected, frontier towns were never humdrum and sometimes entertaining. In one issue of the *Missouri Intelligencer,* Alphonso Wetmore wrote about Mike Shuck, a beaver hunter and trapper who wandered between Franklin and the Arkansas River. Mike's appearance in 1822 set the town abuzz:

> He arrived at this village at 12 o'clock . . . he brought with him from his forest haunts a pet bear, that accompanied him in the double capacity of companion and servant. This animal has been trained . . . to serve with great sagacity as a packhorse, and Mike Shuck, in his advanced age

is no longer forced to bear the oppressive burthen of his traps, beaver, &c . . . I offered [Mike] a chair but he threw himself down on an old trunk . . . while his packhorse [the bear] took possession of the chair.

Panthers and trained bears aside, visitors to Franklin were impressed with its civilized offerings. Franklin boasted an oxen-powered gristmill, a tobacco manufactory, and a rope walk, where locally grown hemp was spun into sturdy rope. The manufactory was set up to process the tobacco grown on farms and shipped downriver to New Orleans. Private schools were opened for the care of the young men and ladies of the town. But the log jail was often too small for the rowdies who floated in on keelboats and canoes. Although it would seem that American soldiers would have protected Franklin, at least during one memorable week in 1822 the soldiers on their way to a fort upriver at Council Bluffs came into Franklin, got drunk, and fought with the townspeople. As if that was not enough excitement, on their way downriver a week later, the soldiers and townspeople once again engaged in a battle. After that, Franklinites voted to improve their jail.

Franklin life was entwined with the Missouri River in ways unmatched by other trail towns. The town grew in the river bottoms, never beyond the sight of the muddy waters. The local farmers raised food crops, but they also tried their hands at hemp and tobacco, and the river's edge was lined with ropewalks and warehouses. The ropewalks were long areas set aside for the spinning and braiding of fiber—usually hemp or cotton—into the long, thick ropes used on wagons, farms, and rafts. Men used simple tools to tie the fibers together into long strands, moving back and forth along the walks, much like a woman at her spinning wheel.

At the warehouses, bales of cured tobacco were graded for quality and stored until they could be shipped to New Orleans. Boonslick tobacco did not rival the quality of tobacco grown in the Deep South or even the Connecticut River Valley, but it represented how quickly the frontier was falling under the control of axe and hoe.

Downriver travel from Franklin was simple: load goods on a flatboat or raft, and let the current do the work. If a boatman watched for sawyers (sunken trees that moved up and down with the current), if the raft stayed upright, if it avoided sandbars and sudden storms, then a man might reach the Mississippi above St. Louis in ten days. From there to New

Flatboats were guided by long oars or "sweeps," and sometimes had a small cabin where the boatmen could cook their food and take turns sleeping. Since the boats could only go downstream, flatboats were impractical for shipping goods for the Santa Fe trade upriver from St. Louis to Franklin, but they were used to ship livestock—and people—from the Boonslick to the Mississippi River. (State Historical Society of Missouri, Columbia)

Orleans and back took several months. Coming upstream was different— keelboatmen could use sails, but they were just as often required to pull the boats upstream by sheer force and strong ropes. If they grabbed onto trees, branches, and shrubs, they were said to be "bushwhacking." No wonder an overland route was more attractive than the rivers. Steamboats were rare in Franklin for many years after the *Western Engineer*. At least one steamboat sank just outside Franklin, spilling more than $200,000 in coins into the river, a treasure that has never been recovered. Not until the river was cleared of snags and logs in 1838 did Missouri steamboats become a common sight. One of the men who surveyed the river for the U.S. Army in 1839 was Robert E. Lee.

The town may have grown up by the Missouri, but the fickle stream was not a true friend. The bottomlands often flooded as the river rose during spring runoff. The wetlands were important to settlers for the game and birds attracted to the water, but swampy areas also created breeding grounds for mosquitoes, which spread malaria. The river was famous for eating up land and trees, leaving its bed as often as a cranky child and carving out new paths through farmland and prairie. The *Missouri Intelligencer* announced in June 1823 that

Hannah Allison Cole was among the first white women to settle in the Boonslick region. She was also the only woman to have a fort named after her (during the War of 1812), and much of her land became the town now known as Boonville. This statue of the "Pioneer Mother of the Boonslick by sculptor Harry Weeks is in the Morgan Street Park in Boonville. (Photo by Richard Schroeder)

From information we believe the late rise of the Missouri exceeds that of any former period since the settlement of the country. Nearly all the islands were inundated, and we apprehend much inconvenience. . . . During its rise an immense quantity of drift-wood floated on its turbid bosom. . . . and so filled up with other matter as to exhibit the appearance of floating islands . . . In fact, we have no doubt that in the long lapse of time, the river gradually changes from bluff to bluff.

The writer may have been amazed at how quickly his prediction came true. In 1826 and '27, large floods damaged and washed away most of Franklin, forcing the townsfolk to move to a place they called New Franklin, but the fickle Missouri River had the last laugh. Many years later, the river retreated to its old channel and returned the site of Franklin to the state. But the Santa Fe Trail did not wait: after 1827, it chose a new home, south across the river.

The Sauk and Fox hunted in the Boonslick region, and were known to the emigrants there. This group of warriors is shown on a visit to St. Louis; the artist was Karl Bodmer, who traveled through Missouri from 1832 to1834. (State Historical Society of Missouri, Columbia)

In February 1810, several families had arrived from Loutre Island to begin life in the Boonslick. Most settled on the north bank of the Missouri in the bottomlands. But two families crossed to the south side— the widowed Hannah Cole, her nine children, the slaves Lucy and Isaac, and Hannah's sister and brother-in-law and their five children. The cold winter had not yet frozen the river. So without an "ice bridge," the Cole family had disassembled their wagons and floated the sections over piece by piece in a canoe, an effort that took several days. The move was slowed by a blizzard, which trapped the family on the river's south side. They survived by eating a single wild turkey that wandered by the camp.

Although these emigrants were the first white settlers to this part of Missouri and founded the town of Boonville, the land was the hunting and camping area of the Fox ("Red Earth People") and Sauk ("Yellow Earth People") who had migrated west from the Great Lakes region ahead of white settlement. The tribes were closely related and had lately lived and hunted in the Boonslick region. Not long after the Coles arrived, the War of 1812 resulted in battles between emigrants and Indians. Eventually, it was the Indians who were pushed north and west out of the region. The introduction of strong liquor, as well as smallpox and other diseases, decimated the tribes. A correspondent wrote of "Indian Manners" in the *Missouri Intelligencer,* on April 1823. A canoe flotilla of Fox and Sauk visited Franklin and Boonville, and the writer strolled through the Indian camp, noting

> very commodious tents or wigwams . . . made with flags or bulrushes, about four feet long and so ingeniously sewed together as to be a complete protection against wind and rain. One long piece placed vertically and supported by poles forms the wall of the building, and two separate pieces the roof. These when [the people] move, are rolled together and are very light and portable. The floors are formed with bark . . . and overspread with bearskins.

It is not clear why the Coles settled on the south side of the Missouri, across the river from other families. The bluffs allowed a view of the bottomlands, and it may be that the Coles felt more protected from attacks during the War of 1812 as well as from the annual river rise and flooding. Perhaps the settlers did not see the Missouri river as an obstacle—after all, they could carve a cottonwood into a canoe in a day or two. During flood stage, the river was dangerous, but it was also much wider and shallower than it is today.

"Hannah Cole's Fort," the only one in American history built under the direction of a woman and named for a woman, was on the bluffs above the Missouri, a strategic location. It was not easy for an attacker to climb the bluffs, so the fort was protected from attack on one side. Lookouts could see across the bottomlands. If attackers set the fort on fire, or if there was a long siege, there was plenty of water. Hannah Cole had built well: the people inside the fort lowered buckets into the Missouri and drew up as much water as they needed.

Early visitors to the region saw an important difference between Boonville and Franklin. Boonville was high above the swamps and the flooding. Titian Ramsay Peale wrote: "Directly on the opposite side of the river [from Franklin] there is the finest situation for a town that we have seen on this river. The base of the shore is a limestone rock which would be long time washing and the soil is excellent with fine water."

An early sketch of a frontier town. As Boonville poet Robert L. Dyer wrote of the Boonslick, "It was a land of salt and honey / where you didn't need much money / But you had to be brave."

Emigrant families helped each other during difficult times. In fact, a toast of the time was "Boonville and Franklin—they smile o'er the waters." But the competition was not always good-natured. On Christmas Day 1819, an early history notes that Franklin "boys" went over to Boonville to "clean it out," and a bloody fight ensued.

Boonville's place high on the bluffs spared it from flooding, and in 1828, when Franklin disappeared under the waters, Boonville became the head of the Missouri Trail. Some folks in Franklin moved their log cabins across the river to Boonville. The town offered traders a river ferry, timber for wagon repair, springs for fresh water, and a direct trail west across the prairies to Arrow Rock. The Cole family ran a ferry service across the Missouri, although on calm days, the river was shallow enough to swim stock and wagons across. Once in Boonville, the trader headed past a small stream called Rupe's Branch and out across the prairie. Boonville played a role in the Missouri and Santa Fe Trails until the 1880s. The town had more than commerce to offer settlers: there was Thespian Hall, where plays were staged, a fairground, photographers, and a singing society. Boonville was one of the few Missouri Trail towns that thrived after the trade had moved along.

Always alert for places to stop and camp—either for the night, or to wait out a flooded river—traders noted areas that offered clear springs, abundant wood, grass and trees for horses, and easy river crossings. Once the men left Franklin, they passed a few isolated farmsteads and an 1812 fort. After a day's travel, they reached a Missouri River ford across from high bluffs. The region was called by French explorers "Pierre à Fleche" (literally, "rock of arrows"). Indians had visited the site for generations to chip or knap the native flint into arrowheads and cutting tools, and the village there became known as Arrow Rock.

William Becknell and his brother operated the Arrow Rock ferry. Here, traders could get information from Becknell about the journey ahead. Because ferries depended upon river and weather conditions, the crossing could take hours or all night. George Sibley wrote that when he traveled to Fort Osage in 1825, a high wind caused William Becknell to cancel the Arrow Rock ferry service at dark, leaving travelers stranded on each side of the Missouri River without food or shelter. Once across the Missouri, however, traders landed on the shore below the town and dragged the heavy wagons uphill. By the 1830s, the village at Arrow Rock was well established and offered traders and travelers a place to refresh themselves and their animals.

A trading caravan could travel twenty miles or more a day, depending upon the weather, the horses, mules and oxen, and the traders' own abilities. At the Huston Tavern in Arrow Rock, built about 1834, traders found food, drink, and companionship. They also found the "Big Spring" or the "Santa Fe Spring" in a small valley to the rear of the tavern. A hard running spring was always important on the trail. People did not yet understand the connection between contaminated water and diseases: ponds and wells were easily ruined by the droppings and urine of livestock or wild animals like beaver and buffalo. And although some people believed that Missouri River water was healthy once the mud had settled in the bottom of a bucket, others knew that drinking the water often resulted in stomach discomfort. But a deep spring could remain pure and provide enough water for thirsty men and animals without fear of cramps or fevers. At Big Spring, stock animals drank their fill, and the men filled barrels for the next leg of the journey to Fort Osage.

In 1807, William Clark, Nathan Boone, George Sibley, and more than eighty soldiers had headed up the Missouri River to begin construction of a frontier military fort and trading post or factory. First named Fort Clark for William Clark, and later for the Indian tribe, Fort Osage was set on a bluff above the Missouri River. The fort contained five blockhouses where soldiers could defend against attacks. Barracks were built around the central square and there was space for the sutler, or the man who provided the soldiers with trade goods and necessities. The fort was surrounded by a log fence and a road led from the river to the entry gate. During the construction, Clark met with Big and Little Osage Indians and made a treaty for their land. Within ten days of starting construction, the men had begun or completed work on the blockhouses, the factory, or trading post, several outbuildings, and a ramp down to the river.

Fort Osage was active until the War of 1812. At that time, the government ordered the soldiers downriver, and Fort Osage was closed from 1813 until hostilities ended. Sibley persuaded the government to open a trading post near Arrow Rock during the war years, but in 1815 he reopened Fort Osage and the next year he brought his young wife, Mary Easton Sibley, there to live. Fort Osage remained open until 1822. Among the visitors to the fort were trappers, mountain men, and the "grandfather" of the American frontier, Daniel Boone. At nearly eighty, in 1815, Boone had set out to explore the upper Missouri River. Accompanied by a man known as Indian Phillips, Boone stopped for two weeks at Fort Osage to recover from an illness before moving on. (In his later years,

Boone took a companion on his trips, so that if he died he would be buried and his family told where he rested in the wilderness.)

Fort Osage became as much a traders' stop as a military fort. Many
traders were white and later, Mexican and Spanish, but the post was
intended for Indians who brought furs to sell and trade. In 1820,
Jedidiah Morse traveled along part of the Missouri Trail as part of a government survey and listed the tribes he met. Morse was a geographer
and a minister from Connecticut, sent by the U.S. government to report
on the condition of the Indian tribes in the West. He had corresponded
with Sibley and spent time observing and visiting tribes of the Missouri
Trail. According to him, by the start of the Santa Fe trade, the Osage
had lost most of their lands in the region and had only 1,200 members;
by 1825, the tribe had been removed to a reservation in Kansas. Of the
Kansas tribe, Morse noted there were 230 men and nearly 600 women,
children, and elders. He also listed the Ioways, who made occasional
visits to the fort, and an Arkansas branch of the Osage Morse called the
Chaneers. Some sense of the Indians' lives near the future Santa Fe Trail
in Missouri was captured in Morse's writings about the Osage and Kaw,
or Kansas, tribes:

> They raise annually small crops of corn, beans and pumpkins, these
> they cultivate entirely with the hoe . . . Their crops are usually planted
> in April, and receive one dressing before they leave their villages for
> the summer hunt in May. About the first week in August they return
> to their villages to gather their crops, which have been left unhoed
> and unfenced all the season. Each family, if lucky, can save from ten
> to twenty bags of corn and beans, of a bushel and a half each; besides
> a quantity of dried pumpkins. On this they feast, with the dried meat
> saved in the summer, till September, when what remains is *cashed,*
> [cached or hidden in pits] and they set out on the fall hunt, from which
> they return about Christmas.

Morse noted that the Indians enjoyed walnuts, hazelnuts, pecans,
acorns, grapes, plums, pawpaws, persimmons, and wild roots such as hog
potatoes in their diets.

Fort Osage welcomed William Becknell and his small trading group in
1821. At the fort, the men wrote letters (and left them for Sibley to send
downriver to Franklin), bought medicine for the journey and took care

of affairs "previous to leaving the confines of civilization." In less than a year, Fort Osage again witnessed something new: the first wagons on the Santa Fe Trail. However, as the trade developed, the end of Fort Osage approached. The traders opposed the competition from the government and convinced politicians to end the factory system. Fort Osage officially closed in 1822, but the Sibleys remained in their home, Fountain Cottage, until about 1827, and traders and travelers continued to stop and camp at the site for years afterwards.

Settlements and towns often bowed to the whim of the great Missouri River. Like Franklin, Independence would become a major trail town only to find itself pushed aside by sandbars and currents. But unlike Franklin, Independence was not stolen by the river and lived to tell its story.

The town of Independence was founded in 1827 and lived up to its name. The town's founders selected a site that was in the woods instead of on the open prairie. Prairie lands were thought to be useless for farming, so settlers preferred to clear the woods and use the felled trees for cabins. One of the cabins was used for the courthouse by day and, according to legend, as a pigpen at night. The fleas got so bad that the court could not do its work, so a brick courthouse was built on the town square.

From its beginning, the town set itself apart. The *Missouri Intelligencer* of June 27, 1827, noted "The Town of Independence is laid out on high, handsome and rich land, surrounded by suitable stone and timber for building, contiguous to never failing spring water; and is believed to be in the most healthy part of the state." Although prairie flies were still a nuisance and mosquitoes were never far away, Independence was not in the swampy river bottoms. It became the last town to outfit traders and trappers heading to Santa Fe and the first to greet the returning caravans. The town answered the need for mules, wagons, and staples such as flour, bacon, and coffee. Blacksmiths, wagonmakers, and wheelwrights offered their services to caravans, and some traders purchased their wagons and teams in the town. Wholesalers and merchants set up shop in Independence, and for several years the courthouse square was famous as the starting point for caravans. But as river travel improved and steamboats made their way upriver, Independence stood to lose much of its trade. When the Big Blue River flooded, caravans were stranded in Independence. Some of the traders headed to a spot called Westport, where they were closer to the Missouri River.

The town fathers of Independence knew that unless they acted quickly, Westport would reap the profits of the Santa Fe trade. River travel was not necessarily faster or safer than overland travel. A boat could be stranded on a sandbar for days, or hit a snag and sink. The boiler could blow up or the ship could catch fire. But steamboats presented one advantage over the Missouri Trail with its mules or wagons: steamboats could carry more cargo in one trip. Independence town fathers decided to connect the town with the Missouri River by improving the landing at Blue Springs, about six miles south of Independence. Soon steamboats were stopping at the Blue and unloading cargo to wagons, which then hauled the freight into the city. To improve service, a mule-drawn "rail road" was built between Big Blue and Independence. But the Missouri had other plans. A large sandbar developed near the landing, and steam-boats once again headed upstream to Westport.

But since the Santa Fe trade had grown enormously, Independence held her ground against Westport. By the 1830s, large caravans of more than 100 men were leaving from Independence; by the 1840s, the city had become synonymous with the trail trade. Not all traders in Independence were American. Mexican businessmen discovered that they could bring goods to the states and export American products into the Southwest, and they traveled between Santa Fe, Independence, and St. Louis. Independence thrived. In fact, it became the most famous town on the Missouri Trail. People came to Independence to watch the caravans leave and arrive from the voyage across the prairie seas. George Ruxton wrote a famous description of Independence in *Life in the Far West:*

> Independence may be termed the "prairie port" of the western country. Here the caravans destined for Santa Fe and interior of Mexico, assemble to complete their necessary equipment. Mules and oxen are purchased, teamsters hired, and all stores and outfit laid in here for the long journey over the wide expanse of prairie ocean. Here, too, the Indian traders and the Rocky Mountain trappers ren-dezvous . . . The wild and dissipated mountaineers get rid of their last dollars in furious orgies, treating all comers to galore of drink, and pledging each other in horns of potent whiskey, to successful hunts and "heaps of beaver."

Early Santa Fe traders traveled overland from Franklin, crossing the Missouri at Arrow Rock. When steamboat traveled improved, it was practical to load the goods onto the boat, ship them upriver, and transfer them to wagons in Westport (near present day Kansas City, MO). The steamboats stopped at Westport because a natural rock outcrop formed a safe riverfront for docking. The wagons and goods were then transferred to ferries and crossed the Missouri River to Kansas territory. (State Historical Society of Missouri, Columbia)

The city watched as what had been an American idea turned into international trade on the frontier's edge. This is what caught Richard Wilson's attention in 1847 as he set off for Santa Fe from the city:

> Here away then we are, at Independence, six hundred miles from St. Louis, surrounded by rolling prairies that rise in the distance to forests of primeval growth, rocking with their green leafy billows, farther and farther, till they seem to make a shore of the bending heavens. This is the great rendezvous of the Santa Fe and Mountain traders, a wild and daring troop . . . all is life and bustle—packing and purchasing—lengthening girths and loading wagons—parting words and stirrup cups—jabbering in Dutch, niggling in Spanish, swearing in bad French, anathemizing some refractory mule in good, long drawn

$500 Reward!

RANAWAY from the subscriber, living in Blackwater township, Saline county, Mo., on Sunday night, July 24th, 1859, the following negroes, to wit:

1st. A negro man named CÆSAR, sometimes calls himself LOGAN, is black in color, aged about 34 years, weighs about 160 pounds, rather quick spoken, sprightly in conversation. No marks recollected.

2d. A negro man, JOHN, aged about 21 years, weighs about 180 pounds, beard just making its appearance on his face.

3d. A negro man, DAN, about six feet high, aged 21, weighs about 175 pounds, with very large feet and blind in one eye.

4th. CHARLEY, about 17 years old, rather tall and slender, weighs about 120 lbs. All four of the above named negro men are black.

5th. A girl, aged about 16 years, low, heavy set, sandy complexion, named ANN; has rather a down look when spoken to.

I will give the above reward of $500 for the apprehension and delivery to me of all said negroes, or $100 each, if taken out of the State of Missouri; $50 for each if taken in the State and out of the county, or $25 each if taken in Saline county.   OSSAMUS HURT,
          Ridge Prairie P. O., Saline co., Mo.
July 29, 1859.

Slaves in Missouri often "self-liberated" themselves, by running away from their owners. A slave could be tracked by slave catchers, whose job it was to stop the runaway from leaving the state for Illinois, a free state, or Kansas Territory. (State Historical Society of Missouri, Columbia)

Yankee—shouts and execrations, laughing and singing . . . attired in buckskin hunting shirts, and moccasins wrought with quills. . . . freed-men skipping around beneath felt hats . . . here a hunter with his gaily painted hat . . . a bowie knife and bullet pouch . . . a blanket. . . . Crack goes the shrill rifle of some hunter; a shout or snatch of song, a rattling of wheels and the first of the . . . train is underway.

Independence may have lost to Westport as the leading trail city, but it retained its Western style long after the frontier had packed up and moved on.

As the Santa Fe Trail grew in commercial trade and importance, it began to resemble a river itself: from the eastern terminus, the smaller routes braided and crossed each other, and then at the western end, the route spread out into a "delta"—the area covered by several ports and jumping off points for the next leg of the trip. Near Independence, Blue Springs to the south and Wayne City to the north provided steamboats with landing places where they could unload their cargo for the trade. By the 1840s, the river landing of Westport assumed control of the trail, overtaking and finally passing Independence. Eventually a landing four miles from Westport grew in popularity over Blue Mills, eighteen miles south, and Kansas City began as a settlement built around warehouses. The small crossroads of Little Santa Fe, or New Santa Fe, also claimed a part of the trade. One story says that a farmer, John Bartleson, built a cabin here in 1833. According to local tradition, he lived on a diet of hominy (dried corn) and potatoes, although chances are he added to the larder by hunting bear, deer, squirrel, and opossum. The village was always small and never became a major point for provisions, trade, or wagon building. Another tradition holds that New Santa Fe was popular for its tavern, which sold liquor to Indians.

By the 1850s, Little Santa Fe had been incorporated as New Santa Fe and suffered raids from bushwhackers and hooligans who were either pro- or anti-slavery. The border wars, as these skirmishes were called, stopped most commercial growth in western Missouri until after the Civil War. New Santa Fe existed only to remind the caravans that they were on their way beyond Missouri.

The End of the Trail

———— ⌾⌾⌾ ————

T HE MISSOURIANS WHO HELPED RAISE the Santa Fe trade from infant to maturity were made of determination and grit. Because the Santa Fe Trail was a commercial venture, more men than women traveled it in the early years. The women settlers of the Boonslick stayed behind to tend the farms while the men set out for the southwest. Hannah Cole sent her sons down the trail, but as far as is known, she traveled no farther than Boonville. Mary Sibley accompanied her husband to Fort Osage, writing her father she saw no white settlers on her trips in 1815 and 1816 to her home on the edge of civilization, and she stayed at her home when Sibley left to survey the trail in 1825. Mary Wetmore accompanied her husband, Alphonso, to Franklin by keelboat and wagon on part of the trail.

Mary Donoho left Columbia with her husband in 1833, the first white woman known by name who traveled to Santa Fe. Thirteen years later, Susan Shelby Magoffin and her servant Jane, a slave, became the second and third women to leave Independence for the southwest. Elizabeth Newcum made the journey in 1847, and Marion Sloan in 1851. Women of the time left few documents to tell us about their lives, but some of the men published poetry, essays, and news articles that reveal the hardships and rewards of the Santa Fe trade.

Slaves accompanied their owners to Santa Fe, experiencing greater hardships than their owners, but the slaves' names are generally unknown. Although the sketches included here introduce only a few of the early trail travelers, historians will continue to discover more stories of the men and women who followed the Santa Fe Trail.

By the 1840s, great changes had come to Missouri. Roads were marked and improved, and steamboats made frequent trips up and down the Missouri River, from St. Louis to Kansas City. Railroads reached across the state. A university had been established in Columbia, and women, as well as their brothers and fathers, had access to higher education. Along with all the hustle and bustle caused by new ideas and technology, the Santa Fe Trail was experiencing changes that signaled its end as Becknell, Wetmore, and other Missourians had known it.

Westport and Kansas City were now the jumping off points for caravans. Although some men still drove wagons across Missouri from the Mississippi to the Missouri, most loaded their goods onto steamboats for the trip. Shipping costs were lower, and more boats reached their destination safely. Outfitters and wagon builders still worked in towns like Independence, but now the "beginning" of the Santa Fe Trail was acknowledged to be Westport, Franklin having long disappeared under the muddy Missouri waters.

The 1840s witnessed the ups and downs of bank panics, tariffs, costs of war with Mexico, and a faltering economy. The lack of hard cash in the West was still a problem, but some tradesmen made the most of it. Messrs. Moore and Porter of Boonville advertised the lowest prices in the town, and in exchange for saddlery, they accepted oats, corn, hay, dry hides, wheat, feathers, wood, bacon, and livestock.

Citizens now enjoyed traveling entertainment and exotic sights. In October 1846, Raymond and Waring's Great Zoological Exhibition came to Missouri on a tour from New York City with an elephant in harness pulling a music car with performers playing favorite tunes! (The parade also included reindeer, monkeys, a cassowary, tapir, lion, and a Santa Fe bear with cubs. Ladies and children were invited to ride the elephant.)

The trade had changed as well. In 1843, Mexican president Santa Anna had closed Mexican "ports" to American traders as a way of preventing New Mexico from breaking away. Although the closure lasted less than a year, tensions between Mexico and the United States had grown. By 1846, war had been declared between the two nations, and the Santa Fe trade would never be the same. Missouri became the home of the Army of the West. This army, under the command of Colonel Stephen W. Kearny, was sent to fight Mexican forces. Although Fort Leavenworth in Kansas was the official "rendezvous" for the troops, many of Kearny's men were outfitted and sent west through Missouri, which provided wagons, food, and teamsters for the military.

While the Santa Fe trade had sent thousands of wagons west each year with commercial goods, Kearny's troops needed hundreds of wagons each week to carry food, ammunition, and supplies for the march. (Kearny reportedly had 300 wagons for his command's baggage alone.) The military turned for help to civilian shipping, or freighting, firms. Russell, Majors, and Waddell of Kansas City was the largest of the civilian freighting firms to move cargo for the Army. At one time, the company owned more than 75,000 head of oxen and 6,200 wagons.

The Army of the West was one of the great U.S. military success stories. By August 1846, Kearny had brought New Mexico under control of the United States. The Army of the West included battalions raised by Mormons and Missourians, the latter described by Oregon Trail historian Frances Parkman as rough-spoken, good-looking men dressed in boots to the knee, "ordinary dress of citizens," and carrying rifles, swords, and pistols. Many of the soldiers had been to Santa Fe—some, like Alphonso Wetmore, were turned away from enlisting because Thomas Hart Benton did not wish to lose important votes by his supporters in upcoming elections.

But greater military strength in the west did not make the trail safer for traders. In 1843, Antonio Charvis of New Mexico had been murdered by a group of Missouri raiders who had deserted the military to become renegades. The murder outraged Americans, but little was done to secure the trail. Although not safer, the trail was still busy even with its dangers. The 1849 Gold Rush sent tens of thousands of men in search of fortune and renewed the importance of towns such as Boonville and Independence. Many Forty-niners followed the Santa Fe Trail to New Mexico for trade, then headed to the gold country of Nevada and California. One story claimed Missouri was nicknamed "The Puke State" because all its men had been thrown out West.

A new form of transportation began: the stagecoach took men to the goldfields, although the shaking and rattling of a coach was little better than walking alongside a team of oxen. Men like Missourian Alexander Majors, who entered the Santa Fe trade in 1848, continued to ship goods by wagon, thousands of tons at a time, but there was little to bring back on the return trip. Mexican silver was not needed: Americans had their own silver mines in Colorado and Nevada. Mexican mules had done their work—Missouri was now the mule-breeding capitol of the world, known for its large, strong, and stubborn animals. Miguel Otero, the Mexican trader, still traveled to Kansas and back, but slowly the trail trade was giving way to other sources for goods, and although Majors and Otero's wagons followed the trail, few followed them.

The Civil War not only split the country, but it brought the Santa Fe Trail closer to extinction. Border warfare between abolitionists and supporters of slavery made it extremely difficult for traders to cross the Missouri and head for Santa Fe. Murders and robberies were common; if any men took a caravan, they did so from the Kansas military forts, not from Missouri.

Beginning in 1863, the Kansas Pacific Railroad and the Atchison, Topeka, and Santa Fe line had been moving steadily towards Santa Fe in a race for dominance. This race would scar the American West. Hunters who supplied the rail workers with meat brought about the near extinction of the buffalo, and Native Americans were pushed farther from their homelands. But the country was on the move and had little time to mourn the passing of its heritage. On February 9, 1880, a branch line looped down into the city, and the first train arrived. The cheers of the population drowned out another sound—that of the Santa Fe Trail bidding farewell to all who had tramped the long, exhilarating road from Missouri to New Mexico.

APPENDIX

The Language of the Missouri Trail

A Glossary

⸺⸺⸺◦❈❈❈◦⸺⸺⸺

THE MISSOURI TRAIL WAS a loud, raucous place, with mules, men, dogs, and oxen braying, shouting, howling, and bellowing, each to his own needs. Harnesses clacked and jangled, wooden wheels and wagon axles creaked and screeched across dips and rises of the trail. On windy days, there was the low whistle of the breeze as it snaked through prairie grasses and threatened to blow hats and canvas to kingdom come. Winter sleet and snow hissed across the plains, and summer locusts hummed in the heavy heat. The people of the Missouri and Santa Fe Trails needed new language to describe their experiences. In some cases, they gave old words new meanings, as with "schooner." In others, the men borrowed words from the Spanish, French, and Indian languages or made up words that sounded as if they should exist. Trail sayings and words like those following appear in the diaries and journals of traders and explorers such as Josiah Gregg, John Fremont, George Ruxton, Randolph Marcy, Susan Shelby Magoffin, Marion Russell, and Alphonso Wetmore.

A good start is worth a day's journey—Traders needed to start well if they wanted to finish well.

Aguardiente—A brandy distilled from grapes. It was also called "pass whiskey" and "pass wine," perhaps after the dangerous mountain passes that led into Santa Fe. Aguardiente was both a drink and an item of exchange.

All's set!—When traders were getting a wagon train ready to leave a campground, each man called "All's set!" to let everyone know he and his team and wagons were ready to go. Josiah Gregg wrote that it was a matter of pride for a teamster to be the first to call "All's set!"

And found—A bullwhacker or other employee was paid for his work on the trail and allowed to take whatever he found or hunted as part of his keep, or food and lodging. So, a man might receive $30 a month "and found."

Apishamore—A saddle blanket or a saddle cover made from the hides of buffalo. The word may have been borrowed from the Algonquins, who used *apaquois* to describe a covering.

Ague—Malaria, a disease marked by violent sessions of fever and then shivering. *Ague* was the old French word for "sharp."

Baile—A formal dance in Mexico.

To bait—To stop for food, generally referring to livestock.

Barbecue or berbacue—open-fire cooking on the trail. The word is from the Taino people of the Caribbean islands and refers to a fire pit.

Barking up the wrong tree—To be mistaken. When a hound chased an animal into a tree, the hound barked until the hunter arrived. But if the game had escaped over the limbs to safety, the hound was "barking up the wrong tree."

Bell nag—A horse that had a bell tied to the rein or bridle. This made it simpler to find the horse. It also meant that other horses followed this leader.

Bit—In Missouri, Spanish and Mexican silver coins were in circulation years after the Santa Fe Trail began. The Mexican coin, or *real,* had a value of 12 1/2¢ and was cut into eight sections or "bits," for convenience in trade. We still say "two bits" to mean 25¢.

Black water or muddy water—Coffee.

Bottoms—The lowlands next to a river. River bottoms appealed to emigrants as farming areas, but the bottoms were places where mosquitoes thrived and spread malaria.

Boudin—French for sausage, but can refer to buffalo intestines, a favorite trail meal when roasted.

Bourge-way—For mountain men and traders, the "bourgeois" or middle class of Eastern and Southern dandies and merchants.

Buffalo chips—The dried dung of buffalo. Often on the trail no wood was available for campfires. But buffalo ate grass, and their dried dung contained compacted grass that burned well. Chips were easy to gather, and light to carry, but one woman wrote she was careful when she picked up chips because of the spiders and scorpions that hid beneath.

Buffalo grass—A low-growing native grass that was a primary food source for buffalo. Later settlers to the Far West used "bricks" of buffalo grass to build sod houses. Another prairie grass noted in trader journals was grama grass, a group of tough grasses that form thick clumps and can provide year-round pasturage.

Buffalo tug—A piece of buffalo rawhide that was soaked in water and tied around a loose joint on a wheel or tire. As the leather dried, it shrank and tightened, holding together wood and iron until a more permanent repair could be made.

Bullion, Old Bullion—Bullion is precious metal valued for its purity and its size, rather than for its face value. A brick (or ingot) of silver was worth its weight in the precious metal, while a silver coin might only have a few cents worth of silver in it, but could represent a higher value than the brick. Santa Fe traders brought back silver ingots, as well as Spanish and Mexican coins with high levels of silver and gold. Thomas Hart Benton, the Missouri senator, promoted the use of hard currency—currency backed by silver and gold, and gained the nickname "Old Bullion."

Bullwhacker—Men who used whips (and strong language) to move oxen along the trail. Bullwhackers walked alongside the oxen, guiding the animals with cries like "gee" (turn left) and "haw" (to turn right). When the simple words did not work, bullwhackers resorted to language not acceptable in polite society. The men were also called "wagoners" or "drivers."

Bushwhacker—To bushwhack had several meanings on the frontier. The word meant to move a boat upriver by grabbing tree limbs and bushes and pulling. It also meant someone who cleared the brush or moved through the brush; thus, a backwoodsman. By the 1840s, a bushwhacker or bush nipple was someone new to the woods (see *greenhorn*). In Civil War Missouri, bushwhackers referred to border ruffians or bush rangers (in Kansas, they were jayhawkers). These men were independent raiders who, although pledging allegiance to a particular political ideal, were often just bullies and thieves. They preyed on the Missouri and Santa Fe traders. Although the word does indicate trees and whacking, it may have come originally from the Dutch term *bosch wachter* or "forest keeper."

By the wars!—An interjection or oath. The term referred to the Revolution and the War of 1812 in which many traders had served, and expressed amazement.

Cache—When a trader or hunter was unable to carry all his goods he might *cacher* (French), or conceal, the items along the trail and return for them later. In most cases, a cache consisted of holes in which the furs or other goods were placed and then covered over to hide their existence.

Camp meat—Game, such as deer and bear.

Caravanbachi or *caravan bachi, chef de voyage*—The former are Spanish for the head of the caravan; the latter is French. The captain of a caravan, elected by the caravan members, whose word was law on the trail, much as that of a ship's captain was on the river or at sea. The *caravanbachi* was responsible for selecting the safest times and paths to travel.

Carry—To lead a horse, mule, or ox. A man who was told to "carry his horse" to the barn was not expected to pick it up!

Catch up!—The order to yoke the animals or hitch them to the wagon and get them ready for the trail. The *caravanbachi* would call out "Catch up!" When ready, the men would reply, "All's set!" and the answer was "Stretch out!"—to move along the trail. Some trail diarists used "gear up" instead of "catch up," but a teamster used only the latter.

Cavallard—A group of horses or mules.

Chapax de braxes—Sometimes words and phrases are difficult to translate because of variations in spelling or because the words were borrowed from languages unfamiliar to the speaker. A *chapax de braxes* was a misspelling of *chapeau de bras* or "arm hat." This was the famous cocked hat worn by Meriwether Lewis. The hats were made of beaver fur brought back by trappers and traders. The Ioways called the beaver *thinye braxge* or thin tail, but this is probably not related to the chapax.

Chapetones (or gachupines)—A white European from Spain in the Americas, who was generally a government bureaucrat or businessman. The word later took on a negative sense.

Chattering like 'coons at roasting ear time—To be noisily talking. Roasting ears were cobs of ripe corn, and raccoons caused much loss of crops in the Boonslick.

Charivaris, shivarees, skimmeltons, and infares—Celebrations were loud and rough during trail days. These words refer to the noisy gatherings outside the windows of newlyweds. Neighbors blew horns and beat on pots and pans until the bride and groom invited the crowd in for drinks and refreshments. A shivaree was also used to drum unsavory folks out of town.

Cibelo—A Spanish word for buffalo. The cibalero was a buffalo hunter, especially one who hunted buffalo for the traders' caravans.

Cold collars—Oxen and mule teams that are put in harness or "geared up" in the morning are said to be "in cold collars." Teamsters knew that the animals would not pull well first thing in the morning, so they drove the animals around the prairie before turning them to hard work, such as crossing a river or climbing a stream bank.

Come out the little end of the horn—To make a big deal about something but have little to show for it. Probably a comparison with a cow or buffalo powder horn, which has a large opening at the base, but a tiny opening at the top where you pour out the gunpowder.

Conestoga wagon, Santa Fe wagon—Heavy wagons built to carry several tons of merchandise in the Santa Fe trade. There is some debate as to whether there was a particular wagon shape called "Santa Fe," but there were variations in the construction of wagons depending upon the builder.

Corned too heavy—Liquor could be made from corn, so to be "corned" meant that one had overimbibed and was feeling the effects of the drinks.

Counterfeit—A fool or a fake. The word was borrowed from beaver hunters, who hid their traps in mounds of sticks and earth built to look like a real beaver lodge—a counterfeit.

Cracker—The bullwhacker added a strip of leather to the end of a bullwhip. The movement of the strip through the air caused a loud snap or crack. (A cracker was a European toy that popped when pulled apart.)

Crease a horse—To shoot at a wild horse and have the bullet barely touch him. This was supposed to confuse the horse and make it possible to capture the animal. Unfortunately, it often resulted in injury and death for the horse.

Deadhead—Slow, lazy animals that contributed little work. A deadhead oxen, when yoked or harnessed in a team, would slow the progress of a wagon.

Dearborn—A small, lightweight wagon with curtained sides used in the early days of the Missouri Trail. These wagons could not carry much merchandise. Dearborns were replaced later by the larger, heavier trail or Conestoga wagon.

Doin's—An activity of interest, such as a meal, a dance, or a fight.

Drive the center—To hit the center or bull's-eye of a target with a rifle or pistol shot.

Equinoctial storms—In the nineteenth century, it was believed that storms occurred at the turn of the seasons, the equinoxes.

Factor—Head of a trading post. George Sibley, a surveyor of the trail, was a government factor. It comes from the word "manufactory" a place where things were made.

Factory cloth—Until the early nineteenth century, women and men spun thread and wove cloth for goods for the home and clothing. But by the end of the War of 1812, shipments of cloth from European factories made life simpler for women. Cloth was an important trade item on the trails. Calico cloth, named after Calicut, India, was brightly printed with patterns. Gingham, a word borrowed by the Dutch from Indonesian, was striped cloth.

Flunk in—To give up and back out.

Foothold times—Early settlement days, when emigrants were trying to survive and get a foothold, or become established on the new land.

Form camp—Many Indian tribes lived, hunted, and camped along the Santa Fe Trail. Some were friendly to travelers, but other tribes were aggressive and saw the wagons and mule trains as easy prey. One way in which traders defended against attacks was to "form camp." The traders would circle the wagons, chain together the front wheels of one wagon and the rear wheels of the next, and then drive the stock inside the circles. In cases of bad weather, wagons could be chained together to withstand strong winds as occurred in tornadoes (sometimes called hurricanes or cyclones).

Fandango—A lively dance and social gathering in Mexico. The word may have been borrowed from African culture.

Forming the camp—Arranging a camp.

Frontier—Land beyond the edge of settlement. The word comes from French, and means the front part of an object or place.

Gee and haw—Words for "right" and "left" used to guide horses, mules, and oxen trains. The terms date to the early 1600s in England, where the driver might say "gee" and "wo," or "gee" and "ree" to control the animals' movements. Bullwhackers preferred "gee" and "haw."

Go wolfing—To engage in a battle and leave the bodies of enemies on the prairies for wolves.

Good leg—The black scout and explorer James Beckwourth called men who traveled despite hardships a "good leg."

Grass freight or corn freight—By the 1830s on the Santa Fe Trail, freight wagons were drawn by either oxen or mule teams. The oxen ate grass; the mules had to be supplied with some corn, which was carried along with the caravan. Oxen were slower but cheaper to use than mules in pulling freight, while mules meant faster deliveries of merchandise to Santa Fe. Thus, to ask for "grass freight" or "corn freight" meant a choice between delivery times and cost for your trade.

Greenhorn or greeny—Someone new to the Santa Fe trade. When cattle were young (and presumably inexperienced), their horns were still somewhat soft and raw (like unripened fruit); these were called "green horns." They had no experience on the Plains; neither did a new trader, thus, the name.

Gum—A hollow stump of a gum tree.

Hold up my end of the log—To take responsibility for one's share of work.

The horrors—How traders described the result of too much drinking.

Hurricane—Sometimes used to describe what we now call a tornado (tornados were called cyclones), the word also referred to areas of trees blown down by high winds.

In the trace—To be kept in line and to follow orders; to behave like a mule in harness.

Jamestown weed—tobacco. The first settlers to Jamestown, Virginia, traded with Native Americans for tobacco. This phrase is somewhat literary; traders referred to "'baccy" or "ambia."

Jerk line—A leather leash that the teamster used to control mules hitched together. The teamster jerked the line to make the mules change direction or stop.

Jerked meat—Fresh meat, usually buffalo, which was dried in the open air, without the use of salt. It could be carried long distances without rotting, making it perfect for travel food.

Jockey stick—A wooden stick attached to the bit rings of two mules who were harnessed next to each other. When the lead mule moved, the jockey stick pushed the other mule to move in the same direction.

Jornada–Spanish for "a day's march." On the Santa Fe Trail, the most dangerous *jornada* occurred as the caravans crossed desert areas, where water holes might be more than thirty miles apart.

Kingpin—The coupling that held together the axle and the pole of a wagon. "Kingpin" still means the most important person in a group.

Kinnik-kinnik—The inner bark of the red willow and sometimes dried sumac leaves, used as a substitute for tobacco by some Indian tribes. Although noted in traders' journals, the word may have been from the Eastern Algonquin tribes.

Konks—In England, your "conk" was your nose or your head. Alphonso Wetmore describes mules "opening their konks" and forcing the caravan to stop for water. The mules may have been flaring their nostrils, smelling for water, braying, and acting restless.

Leader—When a wagon was drawn by mules or horses, the leader was the left front or "near" or "nigh" horse (if you were looking from the wagon to the mules). The swing team was the middle team of mules, and the wheelers were the animals nearest the wagon.

Light goods—Missouri Trail traders were careful to pack many small and light items for Santa Fe. Among these "light goods" were fabric, small articles of clothing, tools, jewelry, buttons—any items easy to fit in the wagon.

Lift hair—Scalp someone. Although scalping was traumatic, men often survived the ordeal and lived to cross the Plains again.

Lightnin' stock—Rifle. Traders and teamsters on the Missouri and Santa Fe Trails carried many different types of firearms, including double-barrel shotguns and pistols as well as the older flintlocks.

Liquor—Drink, often to excess.

Lynch—The execution of someone by a self-appointed group with no legal authority. The term may have come from Captain William Lynch who lived in Virginia and had his own "court" around 1776.

Make a port—Trail terms often reflected the connection that travelers in the West made between the sea and the waving, billowing grasslands and prairies. To make port meant to locate an area for camping. Other seafaring terms taken to the prairie included "schooner" (for the great wagons) and "canvas" (the wagon covers, which resembled sails).

Missouri pistol—Another name for the whip used by muleskinners and bullwhackers. The whips had a buckskin thong attached to the end: these "crackers" snapped in the air, making a sound like a pistol shot.

Mounds, table mounds—Mountains.

Mountain cider—The liquid from a buffalo's gallbladder. These "bitters" were drunk by traders and trappers to cure upset stomachs.

Mulas—Goods that did not sell in Santa Fe were called *mulas* or mules, perhaps because like a mule, the goods stubbornly refused to move.

Mule—The offspring of a male jackass and a mare. (A cross between a stallion and a jenny is a hinny.) Mules were brought back from Santa Fe, but as the trade grew, traders realized that the smaller Mexican mules could not pull the great freight wagons. However, their spirit, strength, and endurance convinced the Missouri traders to import Mexican jacks for breeding and the Missouri mule industry was born.

Muleteer, muleskinner—These men did the same work as bullwhackers, but they guided the mules that pulled the wagons. The muleskinner got his name by being handy with his whip: he could snap a fly off a mule's tail or the head off a rattlesnake.

Nooning—The heat, greenflies, and mosquitoes made prairie travel monotonous and extremely uncomfortable as the day wore on. The flies could drive the stock to stampede or flee into a river or pond to avoid the biting, and mosquitoes could be so thick that a traveler would breathe them in. In order to avoid the worst conditions, wagon trains and pack trains would be up and moving as early as possible. Some trail diaries noted breakfast was prepared but generally the time it took to cook food was better spent on the trail itself. The noon break became the time when animals were freed from their wagons and allowed to graze, and when the men cooked dinner and caught up on some sleep before moving to the evening campground later in the day.

Old corn—Whiskey that was aged, unlike the more raw or unaged "Taos lightning."

On the prairie—Anything that was free or given away. When trading began between men, whiskey might be offered in welcome or "on the prairie." We still say that something is "on me" when we pay for others.

On the lock—Wagon wheels that were stopped or locked up, either by design (to keep the wagon from rolling) or accident (getting a log or obstruction jammed in the wheels).

Osnaburg sheet or Osnabruck—Fabric made from heavy cotton canvas or linen, used to over the wagons and protect the goods and travelers from weather and dust. These were the famous coverings of the prairie schooner. The fabric was named for Osnabrück, a town in Germany.

Out of sight of land—Another maritime phrase, meaning to be at sea and unable to see land. When on the prairie, this meant being out of sight of timber or settlements.

Outfit—This is what made up a caravan, usually wagons, horses, mules, oxen, or other livestock. William Becknell's first outfit was made up of pack horses.

Packers—The men responsible for packing the mules or the wagons during a trail journey. Mules had to be carefully packed or the shifting goods would slow down the animal's pace and, therefore, slow down the caravan.

Paymaster—The man responsible for visiting forts and outposts and paying the troops. Paymasters traveled thousands of miles through frontier territory, and were responsible for any military funds. Alphonso Wetmore was once thrown from a raft and lost thousands of dollars. Despite his small military pay, he was forced to repay the government from his salary.

Pirogue—A dugout canoe, often made from cottonwood trees, could be up to forty feet in length and was able to carry hundreds of pounds in people and goods. The word is French.

Plew—From the French *plus,* with a sense of best or superior. The word referred to the quality of beaver skins.

Plunder—Personal property.

Possibles—The private and personal items owned by a trapper or trader. These could include ammunition, clothing, or utensils. A "possible bag" carried anything a trapper or trader could possibly need or want.

Power—A great deal of something, such as a "power of corn."

Prairie—From Latin and French meaning "like a meadow." A prairie was flat or rolling grasslands.

Prairie bridge–Bridges made of brush or logs, cut down and rolled into soft ground to provide solid footing for men, animals, and wagons.

Prairie fly—Travelers' accounts of life on the prairie mention green, biting flies that could drive animals and men insane. The fly bites could draw enough blood to make an animal too weak to travel.

Prairie wolf—A coyote.

Puncheon—A wooden stake or a wooden slab. Puncheons were used to stake out livestock or to form a walkway over muddy or swampy areas. They also formed the floors in a log cabin.

Purlin—A log or beam in a cabin that supported the rafters.

Rangers—Military men responsible for riding or marching distances, "ranging" over an area. Rangers were usually men with great woods skills, able to survive dangerous and difficult conditions on the plains.

Rendezvous—From French, for a meeting or a gathering of traders to organize a caravan. In Missouri, traders met near Blue Springs where they elected leaders, checked ammunition and packed their mules and wagons. M. M. Marmaduke, a future governor of Missouri, noted in his journal that his group stopped at a place named Camp General Rendezvous before leaving Missouri for Santa Fe.

Responsibilities—Missouri frontier slang for children.

Rio del Norte—The Rio Grande River.

River fever—Malaria.

Rope yarn—A strong, thin rope that could be twisted from buffalo hair.

Santa Fe de San Francisco—Literally "holy faith of St. Francis," the older name of Santa Fe.

Sawyer, snag, planter—The Missouri River was filled with trees that had fallen in or been swept up during floods. The trees made river travel dangerous, whether by steamboat or raft. A tree that had its roots in the bottom but bobbed up and down was a "sawyer," perhaps because it appeared to be moving like a handsaw. A snag was a tree that pointed downriver, so upriver boats would steam or paddle into the tree and tear a hole in the bottom. A planter had its roots "planted" in the bottom mud and the top limbs just below the surface of the water.

Scotch a log—To trim a log of branches and bark. The word may have originally meant to cut or gash.

Set tires—Wagon wheels loosened from all the jarring and bumping along the trail. They would also shrink from heat and require soaking in water so they would swell within the metal wheels. To "set tires" meant to repair the wooden part of the wheel.

Skin boat, bull boat, *beaucoup*—These simple boats consisted of an animal skin tied over a sapling frame, and were used to cross streams but required a bit of practice to use without getting dunked. The boats were more portable than a log raft and could be carried by one person. (*Beaucoup* was a French Canadian term for "very much.")

Skrimmage—A dust up, fight, or confusion. The word is related to the idea of a skirmish, or a battle.

Slantindicular—Aslant or at an angle. This is a humorous word in use by the 1830s.

Slope off—To run away, from an old term meaning to move away at an angle. It was often used to describe sneaky behavior.

Smart—A large amount: a "smart" field of corn.

Snap—A problem or danger.

Sneak hunt—A surprise attack.

Spanish needle—The name of a Missouri prairie, from the plant also known as the begger tick, a wildflower in the daisy family with seeds that have small hooks for grabbing onto animals and clothing. The yucca, which has pointed leaves and bell-like white flowers is a different plant, known as *Adam's needle, Spanish bayonet,* and *Spanish dagger.*

Square up, square off—To take an attitude of someone ready to fight, legs apart and arms raised.

Stampido—Stampedes were one of the great dangers on the plains. Thousands of buffalo or hundreds of horses could cause extensive damage and death in a caravan. Lightning was dangerous not because it might strike a trader—which happened, though rarely—but because it could cause a stampede. Mules were known for their ability to stampede despite complete exhaustion.

Stogies—cigars. The word may have been shortened from "Conestoga," the region in Pennsylvania where the famous freighting wagons were built. Traders enjoyed these cheap, smelly, and sometimes foot-long cigars.

Stony Mountains—An early name for the Rocky Mountains.

Swifter than a streak of pale blue lightning, chasing a switch-tailed salamander to kingdom come—Very fast.

Taos lightning—A strong whiskey brewed in Taos, New Mexico, and famous among bullwhackers. Also called *touse.* See *old corn.*

Taking the back track—Retracing your steps when lost.

Taking the bank—Early trailgoers noted that stream banks sometimes collapsed under the weight of the wagons. In that case, wooden planks were set down for the wagon to cross or the bank was dug away to make for a less precipitous drop to the water. Taking the bank meant to pull a wagon out of the water on the other side of a river or stream.

Teamster—A bullwhacker or muleskinner; a man who manages the yokes and teams of oxen or mules in a wagon train.

Thundergust—A thunderstorm with high winds.

Timber—Trees.

Trace, track, trail, road—These words were often used interchangeably. The Santa Fe Trail was also called the Santa Fe Trace, or the Road to Santa Fe.

Ungear—To halt and remove packs from mules and horses.

Vara—A Spanish measurement, 33," which was nearly equal to the American yard. Cloth for sale in the trade was measured in *varas.*

Videttes—Sentries on horseback.

Water scrape—Any part of a drive or passage where there is little or no water to be found for travelers. The jornadas were water scrapes.

Whereas man—Bankruptcy was common during the bank panics, and legal documents had to be drawn up. A man who lost home, farm, or business was called a "whereas man" after the "whereas" sections of the documents.

Wheelers—Mules or oxen hitched nearest the wagon wheel.

Wind wagon, land ship, sailing wagon—Wheeled wagons or other vehicles rigged with sails. The wagons "sailed" along the prairie at speeds of ten miles an hour or more.

FOR MORE READING

⌬

T HE SANTA FE TRAIL has been the subject of many articles, books, and films. Unfortunately, some of the most interesting documents are not easily available, including news articles from the *Missouri Intelligencer and Boonslick Advertiser* and essays by Alphonso Wetmore. The State Historical Society of Missouri does have microfilm copies of the paper. But there are many classic works that describe trail life and times that are still in print or easily found in libraries. All the books below cover the history of the Santa Fe Trail, from Missouri to Santa Fe, New Mexico.

Bound for Santa Fe by Stephen G. Hyslop (Norman: University of Oklahoma, 2002). A treasure trove of trail history and lore.

Commerce of the Prairies by Josiah Gregg (Norman: University of Oklahoma Press, 1954). Gregg's account of trail life and times is still a classic. His sharp eye and sharper pen provide readers with a look at the birth and growth of the trail in Missouri and beyond.

Following the Santa Fe Trail by Marc Simmons (Santa Fe: Ancient City Press, 1984). The foremost modern trail historian and author of many books and articles, Marc Simmons brings the trail alive.

News of the Plains and Rockies, vol. 2, by David A. White (Spokane: Arthur H. Clark Company, 1996). This series reprints many of the original trail documents and offers biographical, cultural, and historical backgrounds of the men and women who built the trail.

The Road to Santa Fe: The Journal and Diaries of George Champlin Sibley and Others Pertaining to the Surveying and Marking of a Road from the Missouri Frontier to the Settlements of New Mexico, 1825–1827, by Kate Gregg (Albuquerque: University of New Mexico Press, 1952). Professor Kate Gregg was among the first women historians

of the trail. She edited the papers of George Sibley and compiled a
history of the trail's survey.

The Road to Santa Fe by Hobart E. Stocking (New York: Hastings House,
1971). Stocking followed the trail from Missouri to Santa Fe and
beyond, and he tells the trail's history, old and new.

Santa Fe Trail: Its History, Legends and Lore by David Dary (New York:
Penguin Books, 2000). An excellent overview of trail history and the
people who helped shape the way west.

The Santa Fe Trail by R. L. Duffus (New York: Longmans, Green, 1930).
Duffus wrote about the trail with affection as well as knowledge.
This book is still one of the liveliest trail histories.

INDEX

ague, 17, 43, 44, 75, 128. *See also* malaria

Arkansas River, 38, 77, 81, 107, 116

Army of the West, 124

Arrow Rock, MO, 4, 13, 23, 32, 37, 57, 58, 67, 72, 74, 104–6, 114–15, 119

"barking a squirrel," 63

Becknell, William, 6, 18, 22, 26, 29, 30–46, 49, 52, 68, 71, 75, 81, 83–84, 87, 98–100, 114, 116, 123, 135

bees, 15; "white man's flies," 15

"bee bread," 15

Benton, Thomas Hart, 12, 32, 41–43, 45–48, 51, 55, 65, 70, 101–2, 124, 129

Big Spring, 84, 115

bitters, 75, 134

blackjack poles, 8

"blacksnake," 95

black water, 128

Boone, Daniel, 3–5, 8, 10, 13, 25, 61, 63, 107, 115, 127–28

Boone, Daniel Morgan, 32

Boone, Nathan, 4–5, 10, 31, 115

Boone, Olive, 10

Boonslick (Boones' Lick, Boon's Lick), 4–5, 7, 9, 11, 13, 15–16, 18–27, 29ff, 43–45, 61ff, 74, 99, 100, 101, 104ff, 122, 130

Boonslick Advertiser. See Missouri Intelligencer

Boonville, MO, 4, 8, 10, 23, 25, 27, 29, 32, 54–55, 63, 66, 68, 72, 89, 104–5, 110–14, 122, 123, 124

buffalo, 1, 38ff, 47, 50, 52, 57, 58–59, 69, 70, 74, 75, 78–79, 81, 85, 90, 92, 95, 125, 128, 130, 134, 136, 137

bullboat, 79, 136; *beaucoup,* 79

bullion, 6, 129

bullwhackers, 50, 95, 129, 132, 134, 137

bushwhacking, 109, 121, 129,

cabins (log cabins), 2, 5ff, 19, 24–25, 50, 55, 61, 67, 85, 106, 109, 114, 117, 121, 135

cache, 70, 126, 129

caravan, 1, 35, 37, 39, 45, 57, 60, 66, 68, 69, 70ff, 77, 81, 85, 87, 90, 92–94, 99, 102, 103–4, 114, 117–18, 129, 130, 132, 133, 135, 137

caravanbachi, 69, 129, 130

Carson, Christopher "Kit," 52, 72–73, 85–86, 107

chimney, 8, 10–11, 106

chinking and daubing, 8, 9, 11, 12, 106

cholera, 12, 16, 17, 25, 74

Clark, William, 2, 46, 62, 115

clothing, 12, 18, 19, 21, 22–23, 32, 50–62, 77, 98, 99, 131, 133, 135, 137

coffee, 14, 77, 78, 117, 128

Cole, Hannah, 13, 22, 24, 32, 54–55, 110–13, 122

Cole, Samuel, 15, 24

Commerce of the Prairies, 34, 36, 54, 139

corn, 13–16, 26, 40, 51, 82, 91, 116, 121, 123, 130, 132, 134
corn freight, 95, 132
cornmeal, 14
Coronado, Francisco, 3
corrals, 95
cotton, 19ff, 36, 48, 51, 53, 60, 71, 80, 88, 98–101, 108, 135
Council Bluffs, 14, 51, 108
Culver, Romulus, 15, 82
cyclone, 76, 132

Dearborn, 87, 131
Deerskin, 19, 61, 62, 80
dirt dauber, 16
Donoho, Mary, 122
duels, 41–42, 50

factor, factories, 3, 19, 32, 36, 46, 47, 53, 108, 115, 117, 131
fights, 25, 26, 29
Fink, Mike, 28–29
"flash in the pan," 63, 66
flatboat, 108, 109
flintlock, 63, 133
Fort Osage, 1, 32, 36–38, 40, 46–48, 67, 104–6, 114–17, 122
Franklin, MO, 1, 2, 5–8, 12–14, 16–19, 21–23, 26–29, 32ff, 40, 43, 45ff, 64–66, 68, 70, 72, 73, 78, 85, 87, 89, 100ff, 122–23
frock, 20, 21, 61–62

Grand Prairie, 13, 67
greenhorn, 93, 129, 132
Gregg, Josiah, 36, 54, 70–71, 78, 94ff, 127, 139
grizzly bear, 35, 57, 67
guia, 100

Hardeman, John, 6, 7, 22, 50–51
hominy, 14, 121; hominy block, 14
homesickness, 77, 85
horses, 13ff, 31–33, 38, 40, 45, 48, 54, 59–60, 67–72, 74, 77, 79ff, 90ff, 114, 128, 130, 132, 133, 135, 137

hunting shirt, 21, 61, 121
hurricanes, 72, 132

import duties, 100
Independence, 27, 46, 48, 53, 54, 59, 60, 68–72, 89, 96ff, 117–19, 121–22, 123–24
Indians, 1, 2–4, 5, 15, 19, 31, 35, 40, 45, 47–48, 57, 60, 79, 93–94, 105, 107, 112, 114, 115, 116, 121, 125, 132; Kaw, 1, 40, 59, 116; Osage, 1, 35, 48, 59, 60, 116; Pawnee, 1, 48, 60; Sauk and Fox, 48, 59, 111–12

jornada, 75, 81, 133, 138

"keep your powder dry," 63

Lewis, Meriwether, 2, 130
Lexington, MO, 72, 104
linsey woolsey, 23, 62
"looking glass prairie," 99
Louisiana Purchase, 2–3
Lucy and Isaac, 22, 54, 111

"Majors, Russell and Waddell," 93, 124
malaria, 17, 18, 43, 44, 67, 109, 128, 136
Marmaduke, Miles Meredith (M. M. Marmaduke, Miles Marmaduke), 22, 45, 67, 68, 74, 75, 80, 81, 82, 102, 103, 136
marrow, 78
McKnight, Robert, 30, 33, 85
medicine, 16, 37, 43, 60, 75, 116; patent medicines, 16
Mexico, 1, 3, 22, 30, 33–36, 39, 48, 51, 54, 66, 81ff, 91, 99–103, 118, 123, 128, 132
Missouri Compromise, 6, 21, 52
Missouri Intelligencer and Boonslick Advertiser, 5, 23, 26, 29, 33, 35, 40, 44, 51, 67, 73, 107, 112, 117, 139
Missouri River, 5, 12, 14, 17, 20, 27, 32, 33, 35, 46, 51, 52, 70, 73, 79, 80, 97, 104, 105, 106, 108, 110,

112, 113, 115, 117–19, 123, 136

Missouri Saturday News, 69

mosquitoes, 17, 44, 62, 67, 109, 117, 128, 134

"mountain cider," 75

mules, 33, 37, 40, 45, 50, 59, 64, 68, 70, 71, 74, 77, 80, 81, 86, 90–101, 106, 114, 117, 118, 125, 127, 130, 144–50; muleskinners, 50, 91–95, 134, 137

Muster Day, 26, 27

Nettles, 20–21

Newcum, Elizabeth (later Elizabeth Smith), 55, 56, 122

New Franklin, MO, 13, 32, 50

New Mexico, 1, 22, 35, 36, 42, 66, 73, 82, 84, 85, 87, 91, 97, 99, 100, 101, 123–25, 137, 139

New Santa Fe, 121

"nooning," 78, 134

"Old Bullion," 129. *See also* Benton, Thomas Hart

oxen, 50, 59, 70–71, 86, 90, 93–95, 97, 108, 114, 118, 124, 127, 129, 130, 131, 132, 135, 137, 138

Patten, Nathaniel, 5, 51, 52, 67, 83, 107

Peck, John Mason, 17, 19, 25, 71, 75, 76, 107

Pistol, 49, 60, 66, 92, 124, 131, 134, 135

practical jokes, 27–29

prairie, 1, 5, 13, 34, 36, 37, 47, 51, 54, 57, 58, 59, 61, 67, 70, 71, 76, 77, 81, 91ff, 109, 117–19, 127, 128, 130

prairie dog, 38

prairie flies, 48

prairie schooner, 88

quicksand, 89, 90, 94

Quivira, 3

raft, 49, 53, 61, 79, 90, 108, 135, 136

rifle, 12, 19, 21, 32, 33, 49, 57, 63, 66, 67, 70, 121, 124, 131, 133

Riley, Bennett, 43, 49, 50, 70, 78, 93, 94

roads, 88, 124; corduroy road, 4; plank road, 4

saddles, 37, 72, 76, 83, 87

salt (salt springs), 4, 5, 15, 21, 30, 31, 32

salt lick, 30

Santa Fe (city), 1, 2, 22, 23, 36, 38ff, 75, 77, 81, 83, 84, 85–87, 100ff, 125

Santa Fe Spring, 84, 115. *See also* Big Spring

Sappington, John, 7, 17, 43, 44, 45, 102

Schnabel, Amandus V., 55

"scotch a log," 8

Sibley, George, 32, 36, 37, 38ff, 46–50, 67, 68, 71, 114–17, 122, 131, 139

silver, 6, 25, 33, 40, 42, 73, 74, 78, 83, 98, 101, 103, 124, 125, 128, 129

"skinboat," 136. *See also* bullboat

slaves, 14, 18, 21–23, 32, 45, 52–54, 106, 111, 120, 122

smuggling, 100

steamboats, 5, 17, 26, 96, 100, 105, 109, 117–19, 121, 123, 136

"stogie," 89, 137

Storrs, Augustus, 26, 43–47

"summer complaint," 12, 16

tack, 87

thong tree, 4

traces, 2, 3, 4

trade goods, 39, 47, 49, 50, 60, 70, 87, 88, 93, 99, 102, 115

trappers, 2, 3, 33, 62, 75, 78, 79, 80, 87, 107, 115, 117, 118, 130, 134

wagons, 4, 45, 50, 53, 68ff, 70ff, 117–19, 123, 124, 125, 127, 130, 132, 133–38; Conestoga, 87, 88, 89, 90,

130, 131, 137; Santa Fe, 130
wagon trains, 70, 90, 127, 134
War of 1812, 4, 13, 31, 35, 41, 49, 55,
    60, 62, 64, 105, 112, 115, 129, 131
water, 12, 16, 26, 30ff, 38, 74–78, 81,
    90, 91, 112, 115, 117, 138
Wetmore, Alphonso, 16, 19, 22, 25,
    27, 29, 36, 43–45, 49–51, 57,
    60–62, 66–70, 73–75, 79ff, 87, 92,
    99–107, 123, 124, 127, 133, 135

whip, 91, 92, 95, 129, 131, 134
whiskey, 5, 12, 16, 26, 27, 29, 35,
    44, 75, 77, 78, 100, 102, 118, 127,
    134, 137
Williams, Ezekiel, 35, 39, 73, 87
windwagon, 96–98, 138

yoke, 53, 70, 85, 94, 95, 106, 130,
    131, 137
Young, Hiram, 52, 53, 89

ABOUT THE AUTHOR

Mary Collins Barile, a playwright, author, and historian, has written about American cookbooks, the Hudson River and Catskill Mountains, Mark Twain, the Santa Fe Trail, and frontier theater in America. She is currently working on a film documentary about nineteenth-century actress Maude Adams. Mary lives in Boonville, Missouri. She works at the Center for the Arts and Humanities at the University of Missouri.